PRAISE FOR *CE*

"A truly unique book on business leadership because it addresses the critical, practical, and behavioral issues you will face as a leader which are not part of any business theory, model, book, or journal nor covered in leading M.B.A. programs."

—Fred Steingraber, chairman and chief executive officer emeritus of A.T. Kearney

"Over the past 25 years we have worked with more than 70 CEOs in our portfolio companies. CEO Priorities is a must read for anyone who has reached this challenging position or aspires to it. Neil's book provides practical strategies and insights on how to deal with the toughest challenges that face a CEO. This is the first time in our history that we have recommended any book on management."

—Vincent M. Occhipinti, founding partner and managing director of Woodside Fund

"Neil's principles and examples portray repeatedly an old law of leadership physics; that we often select leaders for what they know, when their success or failure depends far more on who they are...."

—Stephen P. Mader, vice chairman and managing director, Board Services Practice, Korn/Ferry International

CEO PRIORITIES

Everything You Need to Know to
Lead and Succeed

By Neil Giarratana

For Brandon from Jeff Lesniewicz
Wishing you and your company
a prosperous 2011

CAREER PRESS

Pompton Plains, NJ

CEO PRIORITIES
EDITED BY NICOLE DEFELICE
TYPESET BY DIANA GHAZZAWI
Cover design by Ty Nowicki
Printed in the U.S.A. by Courier

To order this title, please call toll-free 1-800-CAREER-1 (NJ and Canada: 201-848-0310) to order using VISA or MasterCard, or for further information on books from Career Press.

CAREER
PRESS

The Career Press, Inc.
220 West Parkway, Unit 12
Pompton Plains, NJ 07444
www.careerpress.com

Library of Congress Cataloging-in-Publication Data
Giarratana, Neil.
    CEO priorities : everything you need to know to lead and succeed / by Neil Giarratana.
        p. cm.
    Includes index.
        ISBN 978-1-60163-126-8 -- ISBN 978-1-60163-723-9 (ebook) 1. Chief executive officers. 2. Executive ability. 3. Leadership. I. Title.

HD38.2.G53 2011
658.4'2--dc22

                                                                    2010025454

For my wife, Gabi, who once again showed that love isn't just a word.

~

Most books do not get written without there being a form of "shadow cabinet" behind them; those persons who, over the many months or even years, have worked with the author in discussing with him or her the contents of the book, as well as critiquing the many drafts produced during the writing period. CEO Priorities certainly belongs in this category.

I am grateful to many people who accompanied me on the long journey: Checka Gardner, John Murphy, Jim Drury, Dieter Rickert, Gerry Goldsholle, Alan Webber, Jeff Davault, Bob Swieczkowski, Woody Howse, Dawn Miller, and Miriam Goldberg, who, in addition, kept the engines running on occasion with her fantastic cooking skills. Their words of encouragement, their interest, and, at times, their critical comments, contributed to keeping the writing focused and the points succinct. Others whom I have known and observed from a safe distance managing their own companies, and who "provided" some of the material for this book shall remain unnamed, primarily because I didn't particularly care for the manner in which they approached their leadership and management responsibilities.

A special word of thanks goes to those executives, Alan Hassenfeld, Steve Kaufman, Steve Mader, Vince Occhipinti, and Fred Steingraber, who, in spite of their heavy business schedules and many responsibilities, gave me so much of their time and shared their wisdom by reading what I had written and by discussing with me in such a professional and high-level fashion the contents of this book. I am particularly grateful to them for endorsing CEO Priorities, its goals, and its contents.

Two people who encouraged me to write very early on were Betsy Burroughs of San Francisco, an author in her own right, and

Tom Cafcas, my lawyer of many years. Their guidance and encouragement had a positive impact on my proceeding with the writing of the book.

There are two other people who deserve a particular and special mention for their contribution: my very good friend, Peter Gerber, whom I have known for over 47 years, who, through his own business experience, was always available for a discussion on the one or other point of the book, and who supported my telling it "like it is". And my sister, Patricia Royster, who tirelessly, and for many months, read and reread the manuscript of the book, whose insights and questions concerning the material never ceased to hit the mark, and also whose love of the English language enabled her to teach her brother when he was writing not to split repeatedly his infinitives (here was a good opportunity to do so again!).

A special word of appreciation and thanks to the people at Career Press who had confidence in the book and its message: Kirstin Dalley, Nicole DeFelice, Gina Hoogerhyde, Laurie Kelly-Pye, Michael Pye, and Adam Schwartz. All of them worked in such a professional and impressive manner in moving the submitted manuscript to a finished product and in marketing the message contained therein to the broad book market.

When I started my search for an agent to represent me, I had no idea that I would one day have the distinct pleasure of collaborating with Maryann Karinch of the Rudy Agency, domiciled in beautiful Estes Park in Colorado, who not only guided me through all the necessary and formal steps of writing and having a book published, but also edited this book in such a brilliant fashion. I owe her my deepest gratitude for her professionalism, her patience, her support, and her work. A class act.

And finally, a deep bow in the direction of my wife and my daughters, all of whom spent months tiptoeing around all of the things that needed to be done in the house and elsewhere to give me adequate time to write. And who never tired of asking "Are you finally finished writing your book?" Yes, I can tell them, now I am.

CONTENTS

INTRODUCTION

Wanting to succeed as a CEO is a worthy goal, but to achieve it, you first have to hold on to the job. In 2010, the average tenure of a CEO in the United States is fewer than five years. Contrast that with the late 1990s, when the average tenure of a sitting CEO was more than nine years. While retirement and job changes to another company will always impact this statistic, it is clear that the CEO today lives in a far more complex world with only two givens—uncertainty and change. The discontinuity associated with frequent leadership changes ultimately impairs the ability of an organization to execute a sustainable, winning strategy. Look at the Fortune 500 listing during almost any 20-year period of time, and 40 percent of the companies have not survived as free-standing, independent entities.

The goal of this book is to take you into the real world of CEO survival and to show you ways to avoid or overcome many dangerous pitfalls. You can increase your chances for success as a CEO and your tenure well beyond the current CEO "survival average."

Having street smarts means you can survive on the street, regardless of fierce challenges. What I hope this book will help you develop are your "business smarts." It is often the simplest of issues that hinder leaders in effectively executing their best intentions. These simple problems are not only numerous, their causes are often so well-hidden that the problems have done their damage before you are even aware they exist.

As a result, this is not an academic book on business plans, processes, procedures, or the latest and greatest business models. This is a collection of been-there, done-that insights from a CEO. I designed it as a guide for new and current leaders on how to avoid many of the hidden landmines while putting a strong organization and executing a winning business strategy into place.

Chapter 1

Taking *Any* Road Will Not Get You There

Four critical areas of responsibility take on a character of urgency and practical value when you become the chief executive of a company. These include the establishment of core values, mission statement, a forward strategy, and expression of a vision for the company. If you want to become a successful CEO, you will need to gain not only a mastery of these components, but also communicate their contents effectively to the company's key constituencies, that is, shareholders, board, employees, customers, and vendors. I am going to take you straight to them and talk about some of their most important facets in the cold terms of daily corporate operations.

Business Philosophy: Socrates Is Not Available Right Now

There is nothing subtle about this situation in which you find yourself. Your character is well-known to everyone concerned with who put you in your current position and who has a collegial relationship with you. You have always known exactly where your personal business philosophy belongs: front and center. When you are true to yourself and your principles, others, through the force of your purpose and your personality, also know it implicitly and explicitly.

Most serious companies today have a mission statement to describe what the company stands for and what its purpose is. At times, these mission statements are somewhat too grandiose with their expressions of "being the most successful computer company" or vague references to "creating value." Whatever you think about these language exercises, any *serious* mission statement will also incorporate the core business values the company intends to follow in executing its strategy. This is where your own set of values and your company's philosophy should match up. The core business values function as the company business philosophy. Examine several of the statements of well-known companies with serious core value intentions incorporated into their business philosophies:

- "The high ethical standards represented in these values are expected from employees at every level of our organization."
- "Our business philosophy contains guiding values which are a very real and visible part of our company culture."
- "Our company is customer-focused and responsive to change, balanced by a clear understanding that value and quality guide our decision-making."
- "We take responsibility for our actions. We continually evaluate our business processes to support a user-friendly environment that improves customer and employee satisfaction."
- "We conduct our business with integrity."

How many times have you heard a top executive intone: "As long as I am CEO or responsible for this company, this is the way we will conduct ourselves. My successor can do it the way he wants, but as long as I am here, this is policy." It's king-like, but you get the basic point about the key role of the CEO's philosophy in the company. It counts a great deal. *It drives the functioning of and respect for the core operating values of your company.*

You may find when you move into your new position that a business philosophy for the company already exists. You probably wouldn't have joined the company if its expressed values and purposes conflicted with yours. Should you feel that there are discrepancies in the philosophy or that parts of the philosophy need upgrading, then this will be a priority task for you to address. Your actions will be seen by most of your employees, customers, and vendors as commendable and on-target as long as they seem constructive. But it is still not an easy task to infuse new thinking or philosophy into all corners of the company. How often have you seen employees in the lunch line stop to read the mission statement posted on the notice board in the cafeteria?

Often, philosophical descriptions of personally held or company-propagated beliefs and values will have a nebulous character, which often makes it difficult for employees to embrace them. They will raise questions such as, "What do they mean by that?" or, "What am I actually supposed to do here when I am supposed to be fair/have pride/be morally responsible?" or, "What do these things mean for me in my daily work and life?"

Take, for example, fairness to employees and customers. How do you personally demonstrate your adherence to that value? You may do it by defining what you consider to be a fair agreement in which both parties profit from one specific end result. But do your employees understand what the word fair means for them and their work, even when confronted with your continued fair conduct? Ask 10 people to define, in writing, the word fair when it comes to business, and you will get 10 different answers. Even if you are able to find a definition everyone understands and accepts, you still have the challenge of measuring how much that definition of fairness is actually being practiced in your company daily.

What about integrity? How do people in your company define it? You believe you have integrity and hope that your company conducts its business with integrity. You have been involved in putting into the business philosophy statement that the company must, without exception, act and conduct itself with integrity. But how do you intend to make this word the living mantra of the company and not just a concept with no vitality?

In viewing companies operating with *successful* business philosophies, it is very clear to me that the employees themselves play a central role in determining whether there is widespread respect for, and practice of the company's business values and purpose. The key to their thinking in this fashion is *knowing,* not just surmising, that they are valued and respected as important contributors to company success. They also need to have the opportunity to participate in those company successes through genuine financial reward and recognition of their efforts. If you, the stakeholders, and top management continually underline the fact that your company is successful because it has consistently put both its people and its core business values and beliefs front and center, you will notice that your employees will also work toward making sure their colleagues continue to practice those values.

Encouraging this kind of belief and conviction in your employees represents one of the highest priorities you have as CEO. You should use your annual performance reviews, internal communications, company training, and orientation sessions to showcase the importance of the company's business philosophy. Your constant attention to fostering belief in your company's core business values will help engender an important prerequisite for a serious and successful practice of the company's business philosophy. Never forget that it takes years to build a good name and reputation, but that those coveted attributes can be destroyed by a single major lapse in company conduct.

While the employees play a critical and central role in the widespread respect for and the practice of the company's business values and purpose, it always comes back to you. You are the other equally important factor. It is you and the leadership you offer as CEO, the behavior you inspire and expect, and the values you share that are key driving forces for the acceptance and implementation of the business philosophy of your company. You are the one "riding shotgun" on your company and the conduct of its business.

- If you are proud of what the company has done, then say so. Put pride into practice.
- If you believe that constructive criticism belongs in the mix of any discussion within the company, then make sure your door is open to constructive criticism.
- If you believe that everyone should have a chance to participate in the success of the company, then establish ways to achieve this (everybody contributes, everybody benefits).
- If you believe everything can and should be open to discussion in your organization, then you can, without regret, abandon decisions of the past which are no longer relevant for the future.

Harsh statements designed to promote your corporate philosophy *will* likely only alienate people. Watching you provide value as you tie customers and their loyalty to the company by conducting yourself within the scope of those core values and principles *will* convince people to apply these values in their daily work. Fairness and balance in solving internal personnel or operational problems *will* convince them. Talking with pride about the workmanship involved in the production of your products *will* convince them. Emphasizing the policy of your organization to constantly improve the quality of your products *will* convince them. Voicing disapproval when deviations from the core values of your company surface *will* convince them. Making the required tough decisions, including direct and timely employee removal from the company, to ensure the continued integrity of the company philosophy, *will* convince them.

In summary, there are two essential factors in cementing acceptance and practice of your company's business philosophy:

1.   Leading by example and setting the tone in the company by living the principles and core values set down in the company business philosophy.

2.   Creating a positive we-are-valuable-assets-of-the-company attitude among your company managers and employees toward the company and its business value goals.

To illustrate how important these two factors are, examine their contribution from the opposite side of the equation. In this negative example, it would not be called leading by example, but *destroying by example.* Anyone watching such conduct would see someone sending the wrong message. Do you believe that people are there just to do their jobs, and that you and your managers should manage by exception (only become active when there are operational problems on the table)? Do you believe that negativism, including the use of words like stupid to describe employee performance, is the right way to foster a positive attitude about the company and its principles? Do you believe that concepts such as pride, integrity, or innovation require no further comment or support on your part?

If you want your employees to consistently orient themselves to proactive conduct, and respond to it with matching strength, then remember this: You not only set the standard, you *are* the standard.

VISIONARY GOALS: WHAT YOU THINK YOU SEE IS MOST LIKELY NOT WHAT YOU WILL GET

You want to be special. You want to make a special contribution. You want your company to aspire to making a meaningful contribution to the world.

Some believe that a company without a visionary goal is a company without a purpose. Others will criticize the fact that, if they don't hear people in the company talking about "the vision," then this can only mean they are dealing with a company without a soul.

A visionary goal is not necessarily a *conditio sine qua non* (absolute essential) for business success. Years ago, one of this country's most successful executives, Louis Gerstner of IBM, was asked what he was going to do about redirecting, and thereby perhaps salvaging his new company's fortunes. Included in that question was a reference to what kind of a visionary goal he would favor for the company. The business community waited with bated breath. He smartly refused to be drawn into a debate about vision and the questions accompanying such a debate. Instead, he neutralized the issue by concentrating on the more substantive matters: identifying the means and measures necessary to extract the company from its stagnating and somewhat directionless situation. A vision or lack of vision wouldn't have made one iota of difference in whether this company survived. What this executive taught the business world is the fact that there are times when visionary goals are important, and there are times when they can be counter-productive or just downright untimely.

Visionary goals can be positive motivators for your people and the company, but they can also represent danger or the presence of misguided motivation. The stretch needed to achieve that vision with its perceived lack of credibility and attainability may be too much for many and therefore cause more confusion than good. Other employees, however, can't imagine working in a company without there being a dream or vision of what their company should be striving to reach. They respond to the articulation of that vision; it helps them talk about it and actively dream about and work toward the company achieving it. They are the people who are similar to the last of three groups of workers who were questioned while working on a church construction site. When asked what they were doing there, the first group answered that they were carrying dirt in a wheelbarrow from point A to point B. To the same question, a second group answered that they were involved in putting up a solid building with stone and mortar. The last group offered the definitely more inspirational response: They were building a House of God.

There are companies that suffer under the yoke of a vision that is anything but realistic. It's something that consists almost entirely of dream dust. The discrepancies between the reality of the company's abilities and goals and the vision make the goal statements a farce. In contrast, a genuine visionary goal is a compelling mix of realistic, long-term, strategic goal sprinkled with enough dream dust to make it a viable objective worthy of extra effort and dedication. A visionary goal:

- Can capture the positive long-term effects that your products and company should make to and on your market(s).
- Can be founded upon what the company position should be in the competitive market at some point in the future.
- Caan be based on the contribution your company wants to make to the strength of the country and its position in the world.
- Can reference the quality and uniqueness of your products and their continued value to the customer.

With these thoughts in mind, you can certainly create a visionary goal for your company. However, in order to make your work in this regard meaningful, you are going to need a very clear view, not only of your company's potential, *but also of its limits.* Be careful! It is very easy to blow it right here. In addition to ensuring that the time period allotted to reach the visionary goal is appropriate, confirm that the goal itself is feasible and does not involve you or the company in constant, on-going extreme efforts to make "it" happen. Here are the most important points to consider when you commence work on your visionary goal:

- It must contain a *realistic* appraisal (by you and your people) of the company's current and potential abilities, as well as your corporate culture.

- It must include an in-depth analysis of the relevant critical success factors you will need to shape the future course of your business positively.
- It must include a sound and focused plan of implementation, a strategic plan, containing specific and measurable actions to be taken in order to reach the goal. Make the SWOT analysis (**S**trengths, **W**eaknesses, **O**pportunities, and **T**hreats) the basis and beginning point for your plan's creation.

There is an additional message here: Don't redline your company's and your people's abilities to reach the visionary goal you have chosen. Instead, dream the dream, but stay real. Contrast in this regard two visionary statements from two totally different companies. Google's powerful visionary goal is only nine words long: "To facilitate access to information for the entire world." This kind of goal represents an ongoing vision to provide the world with an ever-growing amount of information. It is a dream, but a realistic one, because the company is moving closer to that objective. Its overall company strategy is focused intently on this goal. Compare that to the "visionary" goal of another company: "To be the nation's highest quality and most successful health care enterprise by 2010." This visionary goal was valid as of the middle of 2009 at a time when this company wasn't even on the Top 20 list of *U.S. News and World Report's* listing of top U.S. hospitals. No realistic vision or dream here; therefore no need for a reality check.

There is nothing wrong with pushing hard at the limits of what currently characterizes your organization in terms of market position, internal capabilities and talent, and positive drive. This is part of your job. But just like people, companies need breathing room in order to develop properly. Excessive and constant nudging of people to push hard toward an unrealistic visionary goal isn't going to do it. It's particularly hard to swallow when you have created a visionary goal for your company that you believe will not only benefit the stakeholders' position, but also society at large. Just don't forget to ascertain how you are going to get the company to climb the huge mountain that exists between its present position and its visionary goal.

Keeping your passion in check is part of ensuring that that goal remains realistic and doesn't become counter-productive. However, once your vision, as well as the strategic plans necessary to achieve it, have been clearly defined and accepted, it is perfectly legitimate for you to do what is necessary to continue to make that vision credible and real for your employees. You will want to continue selectively referring to it in your discussions with company personnel or with the board. You will want to write about it in the annual report, talk about it in interviews, and refer to it at times at the beginning of one of your speeches. It is a priority job for you to ensure that that the visionary goal remains credible and achievable in the eyes of your people.

Dreams and companies *do* go together. In rough times, visionary goals can be distracting, as they can be viewed as ethereal appeals. But a smart CEO knows how to weave and keep alive the dreams of the company both in good and in challenging times. Modulate your efforts according to those times, employing different strategies and adjusting your approach as appropriate. Intent and finesse *also* go together.

THE BUSINESS COMPASS: WHY THE NORTH STAR NEVER MOVES

Magnetic fields cause a compass to spin or to point in the wrong direction. In the business sense, these fields have a much more insidious character: They involve temptations, shortcuts, lies of convenience, selective acceptance of regulations, greed, short-term thinking, compromises, falsification, cover-ups, use of indirect or direct coercion, and even blackmail. While there are many companies that exhibit exemplary conduct, unfortunately, there are others that do not.

People who play in this kind of world commonly exhibit the most dangerous of mindsets, namely, Teflon thinking: *Others get caught; we're smarter.* The world in which they operate represents a moral void. Regulations, rules, and propriety enter that space so briefly that they hardly show up on radar. Imbued with this attitude, such people show pride in maintaining that they can put a toe over the line occasionally and not get caught. They ask themselves rhetorically: *Even if we get caught and the company has to pay a fine, what is that compared to all of the other things we've gotten away with in the meantime?*

The lack of integrity may not be obvious—even to the people closest to them. Such executives scrupulously fill out every tax and reporting document required by law, register with the Securities and Exchange Commission and do all that this regulatory agency requires, speak publically about their devotion and allegiance to the law, and espouse the fact that their company runs a tight and clean operation. But their minds allow them to live in world where these actions are like paint on a rotting picket fence. No one really sees the difference, even when viewing that fence close up.

Their general thinking is: *We are basically a law-abiding company (and I am basically a law-abiding person), but certain laws and rules are stupid. They should be repealed. While rules and laws are generally important to us, they have to be bent occasionally when certain demands arise in the course of our doing business. We will adhere (mostly) to the letter of the law, not the spirit of the law and that gives us a little wiggle room to play things the way we feel they should be played.* What they say publically is different. There is a risk to this way of thinking. Often, it doesn't work as well as management thinks it will. Regulators and whistleblowers don't think that way.

As the world has recently seen, management's selective adherence to the letter of the law and not abiding by its spirit cuts across a whole spectrum of companies. Average people get scowls on their faces at the sound of names like Enron, Toyota, Lehman Brothers, Massey Mining, and Sunbeam. In addition to public scorn, consequences include a severely damaged reputation, legal and tax implications potentially leading to jail time, or in the case of the mining company, death of its employees. These are also consequences that directly affect the very existence of the companies involved. Enron, Lehman Brothers, and Sunbeam no longer exist in the form they once did. The others have become targets for investigations and censure.

There are two priority issues for the CEO to consider in this area of corporate morality: the definition and the application of personal integrity.

First, in carrying out your duties, you will very likely be faced with moral challenges—they are almost inescapable in this complex world. The title of CEO means total operational and leadership responsibility, and challenges and temptations come with the territory. While you may never have been tested or tempted to stray in the past, you are now in a very different game.

This reality requires that you devote time to communicating with your inner-self and preparing for those temptations. Know who you really are and what you stand for. Reflecting on this subject does not mean doing so when actual situations arise in which you will have to make an immediate call or play. You need to know *in advance* what kind of morally responsible human being you are before you are confronted with a borderline situation, and how courageous you will be, should you find yourself in such a situation.

Second, know how you intend to shape your employees' standards of conduct of the company's business. Officially, you will want to include the details of your thinking in this regard within the body of your company's mission statement. However, in daily practice, part of your plan to support this endeavor will include paying attention to and focusing on *what you say and do*, thereby visibly underlining the importance of ethical values for everyone around you. Others' respect for you, and your respect for yourself—these are the valuable assets that cannot be sacrificed on the altar of need or greed. If you were a decent person before, don't let power become your drug of choice and kill your integrity.

Assuming that you personally have a functioning moral compass, you can then proceed to the remaining equally important issue revolving around how your personnel conduct themselves. It is a fact that sometimes far-flung divisions and managers do not always have the same principles and standards you do, particularly if you lead a highly diversified international company. How do you ensure that they also have done some of the same kind of serious and reflective thinking? You can work at cultivating a sense of morality in them by conducting in-depth discussions of such principles during staff and department meetings, as well during annual personnel reviews. To ensure that these discussions maintain their relevance to daily operations, you would couch their content within the framework of your company business model and your company's forward strategy.

Whether you like it or not, you are responsible for setting the example across the whole company when the company is confronted with morally difficult and therefore dangerous situations. And if you discover or suspect that certain people don't share your principles, and their actions subsequently confirm that opinion, then you won't want to hesitate in your decision: This is unacceptable conduct and has no place in your company, nor do the people involved.

Minor aberrations within a particular department can occur occasionally. They do not represent a serious danger for the company. However, if you and your management team don't reinforce official company policies on correct conduct, and if you don't consistently watch for such transgressions, they will continue unchecked, and may even grow in number. An even more serious danger is being asked to approve something out of line "just this one time." This can sometimes occur in a non-formal setting: Someone takes you quietly aside to get your approval on something. If you go along, don't think that such behavior on your part will go unnoticed or not be mentioned by your employees when other similar issues arise. One misstep, and you have given away part of your moral authority.

Even though you may have incorporated all of the right values into your company's mission statement and personally demonstrated your respect for those values, your work in assuring effective practice of these values is just getting started. Statements relating to these principles in the personnel handbook, the speeches you give, or the discussions during annual personnel reviews always help in reinforcing the message. But "reading" your company, really seeing what could potentially come back and bite you and/or the company, or the stakeholders, that's what counts and it's not an easy task. Look for subtle warning signs, as well as for the obvious egregious conduct that could be taking place:

- Continual over-emphasis on the part of your managers, both verbally and in writing, to you and the company that the law and all regulations are being observed. Think back to Shakespeare's *Hamlet* and the observation that someone "protests too much" to be believable.
- Repeated denial, or even condemnation, of rules and regulations of the company or the government, as well as references to how stupid these regulations are and how they get in the way of doing business.
- A request to top management to look the other way "just this once" so the numbers will look good. If one of your people is asking for such a major step this time around, it could mean he or his department may have done other smaller questionable things previously

without asking. And even if you should say no to this overt request, how do you know that these "smaller" transgressions won't just continue in the future?

- Push-the-envelope questions from divisional or subsidiary CFOs to your Corporate CFO. While the law is very clear on the liability of management signing off on the results of the company, such questions could imply temptations or even directly indicate your people are considering taking certain reporting risks when they submit an application or financial data to the regulatory authorities or financial institutions.

- Consistent late arrival of monthly reporting results and/or yearly audit material containing mistakes and fuzzy cost or revenue allocations or computation.

- Resignations of key people you respect at divisional or national subsidiary level without any clear reason, or for reasons you consider false.

- Activist-like group activities against the company. Legal threats or legal procedures against the company or a particular division.

- Internal revision reports containing information on the lack of application of standard risk management principles and policies. How often do you receive memos or letters on the same subjects applying to the same problem areas or divisions?

- Required annual revisions of audited results as well as the contents of the auditors' Management Letter as it relates to company divisions and their "good practices."

- Demands by the responsible manager that the same person or people who did the audit previously be part of the team conducting the audit again this year. Watch the length of time the same auditor or team of auditors has been involved, as well as the intensity of the request itself. While a new legal obligation requires that the auditing firm replace the individual partner responsible for the audit every five years, this still could mean that the audit team itself may be exactly the same one that has worked on the account for years. Tyco International stands as one of the most brazen examples of misuse of company assets in recent memory—and this is in a company that was audited every year.

- Auditor office presence in the same building as the company offices. Unacceptable.

- Apparently indiscriminate firings of several managers by a senior or middle management person without any identifiable cost-saving necessity or performance-related problems.

- "White glove" tests for inventories during warehouse visits. If the glove fingers turn black, you may be looking at old product where the necessary write-downs, for the *wrong* reasons, may not have been taken in a timely or correct manner. Exception: Warranty parts being kept to provide availability of discontinued parts or product to your customers during the warranty period.

- Gift-giving to local VIPs beyond what might be considered acceptable in the respective company or country culture. Your company policy must have clear and defined instructions and limits on this kind of activity.

- A significant lack of any visible financial costs, fees, or sales commissions (as far as the company allows them to be *paid)* in divisional reported numbers, meaning that off-the-books payments could be taking place. As a corollary, if you visit a company subsidiary and are welcomed like a king and, in addition, introduced excessively to local officials, take a very hard look at the reception committee's operational results.

- Special deals or extended payment plans for several customers without recognizable need, which go way beyond normal company customer practice.

- Booking of payables and their payment may be organizationally too close to one another, or even being done by the one single "trusted, long-time employee" of the company. Missing checks and balances in this area may prove to be a formal invitation to those so inclined to embezzle funds from the company.

- When demanding back-up data for certain costs or expenditures, hearing excuses that the data is not available or the staff person who did the analysis and was responsible for this area has left the company so the numbers can't be verified.

- Extreme life-style differences within your management group that could raise the question of income you do and don't know about.

Does all of this sound far-fetched? Far from it. Do not ever underestimate the creativity of those who have their own agenda, or who simply want to beat you at the "game."

Some of the responsibility to uncover such aberrations lies clearly within the scope of the work of your auditing firm. The relationship between your company and your auditing firm should have a formal arms-length character to it. And you should not be involved in the selection in any way. However, the auditors come from outside and are usually involved in formally auditing your books only once a year. You also need continual and consistent control *inside* the company if you are going to recognize some of the more serious issues. You should therefore have an Internal Revision Manager, whose responsibility consists of questioning everything and anything having to do with the company, its practices, and its financial results. This person should not report to the Controller, but to the Chief Financial Officer only.

The financial controls you have established, giving you an overview of the performance and financial viability of the many parts of your company, represent additional support in stopping or blocking any excesses. In addition, be sure all of your executives and employees sign a company code of conduct containing those principles that guide the company in its business and in its relationships with its total environment. Put those documents in their personnel files and review them once a year, particularly with each member of your management during their performance reviews.

A number of the compasses in today's business world are off-kilter. You certainly don't intend to abandon the principles you know are appropriate to guide the conduct of your company. The activists, regulators, or legislators coming through the front door of your company aren't going to stop first to see if you have fresh doughnuts in the company cafeteria. In the interest of the stakeholders, your many honest employees, your customers, and your own position, you must regard the task of identifying and eliminating such problems as one of your highest priorities.

GROWN-UP MODEL BUILDING: THINKING YOU ARE GOOD DOESN'T MEAN YOU ARE

Let's define a business model and what it should accomplish. The classic definition describes the operations of a particular business, including the components of that business, its key functions, and the revenues and expenses that the business generates. On the operations side, is the company a manufacturer of consumer non-durables, for example? As a corollary, does it have products possessing a specific uniqueness, and therefore offering a specific value proposition? When you turn to the functional side of the equation, there are two important components involved for business model success:

1. Does the business model produce or create value, defined as a particular product or service going through the manufacturing process until it is ready to be sold?

2. Does the model provide the framework for that particular product to become a unique resource or asset to the person or company using it?

Business model design means defining the business of the company at the strategic level. Thus, a business model will include the following elements: a discussion of the company infrastructure, its product or service offering (value proposition), the customers or customer segments it seeks to satisfy, the channels of distribution to be used to reach the relevant customer segments, the customer relationship and the management of that relationship, and the cost and revenue streams.

Today, the strict definition of the business model has broken down. In many cases, the term now applies to a broad range of informal and formal descriptions used to define core aspects of the business, including purpose (definition of what the company does), strategies, infrastructure, organizational structures, trading practices, and operational processes and policies. In even more simple terms, it describes, in clear fashion, how the company makes it money, and how the company intends to grow its business in order to earn more money.

A business model must be clearly identifiable to all who come into contact with it or work for the company. Its market and economic relevance must be recognizable. Its consistent application provides proof for just how cohesive and focused the company's management is in the operation and execution of the company's business. An appropriate business model does not evolve in a single day, but after much discussion, reflection, and practice, the model develops over time into a standard by which the company conducts and practices its business. There is no question that long-term business success comes from building and then maintaining a winning, always fresh, and up-to-date business model.

Particularly important for the relevance and success of a business model is this: Smart CEOs will know the ways in which their businesses are different from those of the competition. They will have shaped that difference and will emphasize those differences at every opportunity, as well as push and innovate to *maintain* those differences so they remain unique for the company's target markets.

As CEO, you know the formal and somewhat less formal framework of a business model or business model design as it is used today. You have worked within several models on your way to your current position. Clarity and uniqueness in your company's business model reflect how effective *you* are in shaping and forming your company's business and its future. Your business model must do the following:

- Provide a detailed picture of why your business does what it does and why, and in maintaining that particular way of doing business, the company will achieve success.
- Make economic sense in terms of the stakeholders' established financial parameters and aspirations.
- Be market- and customer-oriented. The principles contained therein must have long-term sustainability. The value proposition must be apparent and credible and, above all, reliably and consistently deliverable to the target groups indicated in the model.
- Prompt management to ensure that the right people are in the right positions in order to create the optimal preconditions for the execution and success of the business model.
- Be so relevant and compelling in its message and objectives that the vast majority of your high-potential employees will want to commit to making its execution an overriding success.

- Communicate in such a way that each and every one of the people employed in the company can readily understand what the company does and how it intends to keep on doing what it does. Your employees must appreciate where the major elements of your business model differ from those of the competition. In addition, they must recognize how those specific competitive advantages, if properly supported and executed by them, will impact the company, themselves, their income, and their job security.

- Provide feedback to you and your top management that indicates how effectively you are communicating the model throughout the company. Some of this feedback can come to you through personnel reviews or quarterly or annual review sessions. But you and your top management should also be able to recognize, simply by observing and listening, how solidly established your company model is in your employees' approach to their responsibilities in the company. In addition, results that reflect successful execution of the employees' duties offer further confirmation of the fact that the model is understood and is being used appropriately. If all of this is a little too much for you, then try the Blank Sheet Test. Ask your top 20 people to write down on one sheet of paper what they think the company is doing and where it is going. Main idea: Define what we do. The result will most likely be answers in many different directions. The end result is that nobody knows what is really going on. Conclusion: You are not doing your job.

A key priority for you as CEO is to set fixed periods of time on an annual basis when the whole company business model will be formally reviewed and, if necessary, redirected to reflect changing conditions in the company's environment, or to mirror a basic change in the strategic direction of the company. Call it an annual checkup. This necessity is important for a number of reasons. First, your management needs a regular refresher course on the intents and purposes of the company. Operationally, the needs and buying behaviors of your target/customer segments may have changed, so that your current "unique" product philosophy and value proposition may no longer fit well in the market. Secondly, the company may have decided to integrate vertically or practice lateral diversification to ensure further growth, thus requiring a change in the way the operations and functions of the company are currently structured. Thirdly, the company's product line and the channels of distribution used to sell it to the market may have changed so much in content that new and different distribution and sales activities are required. Changes in the economic environment or advances in technology may also be affecting your business model. In addition, competitors tend to try to replicate or even trump a highly successful business model, thereby forcing you to strengthen or to change the tenets of your model. Often your competition becomes increasingly successful in its efforts to do this, thereby negatively affecting your company's potential in the market. Ted Levitt, former Professor at the Harvard Business School, spoke of how pioneers lived dangerously because they tended to get killed by the Indians. Tie this statement to your current business model and check for its applicability to your situation going forward.

Finally, the size and attractiveness of the market segment in which your company operates may have been negatively impacted. Consider the story of the buggy whip company and the arrival of that loud contraption called a car. As a result, you should constantly be looking for new markets and new perspectives for your company.

It is a fact that business models do not have extremely long lives. You may like things to be clean and neat, but the business world is not. Ensure that your company business model remains *current and credible*, adapts itself as necessary, undergoes continual and critical examination, is recognized by your people as the motor of the company, continues to emphasize uniqueness and differences in your company and its products, and doesn't develop a lot of rattles.

Critical Success Factors

The major building blocks of your business model and the strategy that underlies it should be the subject of periodic discussion with your board of directors. Strategic oversight is one of the board's most important functions and responsibilities. Draw on the board's experience and point of view.

In any strategic or operational workshops held in the company during a running year, the model and its major points must be part of the agenda. Frequently remind your employees of the major facets of the business model and its applicability to what they are doing. Encourage them to comment honestly and openly on the model and its continued appropriateness and suitability for the company.

In order to ensure continued appropriateness, you might decide to form a committee made up of key management people who would meet semi-annually, or even more frequently, if there is the need or potential for major strategic change in the near future. The committee's charge would be to provide an ongoing review of the model's contents as well as the strategy behind them. In addition, it would provide a semi-annual report relative to the current state of the company's model and make recommendations involving any potential need for redirecting or revising the model's contents. Their work would be included in the detailed review of the model you would conduct every year.

Refer to the model in your daily work. This means citing its contents, their applicability, and their relevance for the company in your decisions, daily discussions, or speeches and short comments to both company personnel and people outside of the company. This approach has an important practical side to it. By frequently talking about the model, you will be reviewing and reassessing its contents in your mind. When you talk the model, you will talk the logic of the model. In doing so, you will indirectly be comparing the reality of your company situation to its current business model. That kind of comparison could very well lead to noting and then initiating a rapid revision of your business model. Make this change official without waiting for your "Committee for Model Integrity" to meet or for the Annual Strategy Sessions to take place where the model, its definition, and applicability to the market are, of course, always on the agenda.

From time to time, select a single subject or tenet of the model to highlight in your ongoing impromptu discussions, meetings, or formal gatherings with your employees. There is nothing wrong with sharing stories about experiences you have had that humanize or stress the importance of a particular part of the model and its functionality or, conversely, possible loss of functionality. There may be an occasional Oh-no-here-we-go-again reaction from those who may possibly have heard these experiences before, but these examples serve a useful and enlivening function in sensitizing your people to the model's continuing importance—and the possible potential for a change in its content.

Deviations or damage-to-the-model issues arising within any particular department of your company should not be handled in the form of a kangaroo court. Instead, encourage your people to review such instances with you. There might be a need to readjust the model as a result of specific actions taken to get a job done. These non-conforming actions could potentially indicate inherent weaknesses in the model and should not be discarded out of hand or punished; they contain value.

The greater the detachment that the people in the company have from company headquarters, the greater the danger that the model will be altered, ignored, or only partially applied. This maverick approach is often particularly evident if the company is structured in a more decentralized form. No business model can completely eliminate the dangers of fiefdoms and what they will or will not do with a company business model. Your job is to ensure that each and every responsible member of the top management team, wherever located in the world, has had his initial inoculation and that he gets his booster on a regular basis.

The CEO should pay particular attention to the company sales force and how it projects the business model. Sales people should be communicating the basic elements of your business model to potential as well as existing customers. For example, if part of your business model involves selective distribution within a specific channel/target group, then this fact certainly possesses a key and direct value for the customers carrying your product. Unfortunately, many sales professionals are not always good at introducing and then discussing the model content and its relevance for their customers. Many of them don't even know the principles or concepts involved. They want to talk product and terms. What they *should* do, particularly at the start of a new customer presentation, is prepare the groundwork for a sound business relationship. This would entail, for example, your sales people giving the customer a feeling for the unique value of the company's business model as it pertains to customer relationship management, or how the model's tenet on selective distribution will directly impact the customer's potential for success in the market.

The smart CEO will ensure that the sales group focuses not only upon the sale itself, but also upon creating optimal preconditions to making sales by convincing customers of the uniqueness and strength of the business model.

Do not minimize what is really in play here: Every customer wants to feel confident that your business model has long-term viability so that the customer can *build his business around your business.*

If you really want to test the internal core of your business model and its relevance, then consider the following scenario and question: Pretend you are getting ready to leave the company and go elsewhere within your industry. (For purposes of this exercise, you don't have a non-compete clause in your contract.) With what means and strategy would you compete against the company for which you currently work?

In beginning to answer such a question, you will observe not only the obvious, but also the *hidden* weaknesses in the model that you are working hard to eliminate. At the same time, knowing the internal situation as you do, you will also recognize that some of these weaknesses are not going to disappear overnight. For example, the product line may be losing its attractiveness, the value proposition of your services may be weakening, or your customer segmentation may no longer be valid, causing ineffectiveness and higher costs in your efforts to sell your product. These are weaknesses within the model and its implementation that your competition hasn't quite seen in its scope. But you know that if you were on the other side of the fence, you would spot them and exploit them. There's nothing like reversing the situation in which you are the competition to gain a new, and perhaps troubling, perspective on the situation in your company and on the relevance (or lack thereof) of your company's model to its environment.

As a result of this exercise, you may in fact discover that the "great" business model you have is less than optimal for providing the platform for that top-priority responsibility you carry with you every day: growing the company and its value on a long-term basis.

Key Priorities

- If you have a great strategy for your company, you need to define it in detail, and transfer to your employees the company's core business values, which will accompany and impact its execution.
- Visions represent a look into the far future. They are something you aspire to realize and they can be dangerous. Don't redline your

company. Know its limits and what you can demand of it, both in its current state and in its planned future state.

- There are potentially more bad things going on in your company that you don't know about than those you do know about. Your integrity and your watchfulness are of prime importance in reversing this situation.

- Fuzziness in your business model and in your company's approach to earning money could cause your company to become second-class. Your constituents, that is, board, shareholders, employees, and business associates must have a clear and fundamental understanding of why a company does what it does, why it does it that particular way, and what the result should be.

Chapter 2

YOU SELL SOMETHING— SO GET IT RIGHT

Timeliness, reading emotions, making sure your product or service functions properly—these are just a few of the key themes that cover the most important thing you do: selling to and serving your customers. You can't do that well, of course, unless you have an intimate understanding of how your sales force and your customers think, and what their respective needs are. Once you find the right salespeople (and I will tell you how to do that) you need to understand what their world is like, so you can support their efforts effectively while mitigating their frustrations.

BORN TO SELL, BUT STILL NOT A WALK IN THE PARK

The world is nothing but one big sales function. Your agenda, their agenda, products, services, programs, methods, progress, politics, government, opinions, counter opinions—you name it, everything is on sale or being sold. It is the buzz in everything that goes on in our daily lives.

In the business world today, the selling function is high science. Focus groups find out what people want or like or don't like. Software tracks surfing activity and draws conclusions on preferences. Retail sales stores use subtle advertising and product merchandising to entice the purchase decision. Soda dispensing machines dispense drinks and simultaneously pass the choice to a central gathering point for analysis. Some would say we don't have a chance: We are already buying. We just don't know it yet.

The one potential element of sanity in all of this is the sales force out in the field, one foot in front of another, forever hopeful that the next call, visit, or contact will bring that familiar jolt of success. Generations of sales professionals have come and gone and still, in spite of every advance in selling in our modern age, there remains a need for two human beings talking about a product or service and its uses.

There are no machines at work in selling. There are no exact or dependable formulas for success, which, when applied, will produce the desired sales result *without exception.* Selling is a complex activity. During the course of your career, you will have had either direct or indirect experience with one or several sales groups. You know that in any face-to-face sales activity, the driving and central factor is the human being with different personality, character, and emotions. The result is rapid fluctuation between highs and lows, enthusiasm and frustration, and superior and haphazard sales performance. Certainly, there are macro-economic factors that will affect sales success: recession, industry-related difficulties, or internal financial difficulties for your major customers, which negatively affect their ability to buy. But these are elements of the equation that can at least be forecasted, and therefore taken into account when setting your company's sales goals.

As CEO, you must be directly involved in your company's sales activities. This would include influencing not only the overall policies, procedures, and functional attributes of the sales operation, but also having direct contact with your customers. This is a world you must study, respect, and cultivate. If you do not understand this world, you run the risk of misjudging or misusing your sales force, and the investment your company has made in it, thereby creating serious problems where none existed before.

Why is it that you hear the word frustrating when the sales experience comes up in conversation? The highs should be clear enough to you. But even if the product is good or even exceptional, you still need to understand where all of the frustrations come from, and why they exist, if you want your sales groups to work successfully and achieve optimum performance levels.

What is the real selling world?

People doing the actual selling operate in an area where opinions, feelings, thoughts, and memories influence the responses of the person with whom they are speaking. Many of these situations are unique; the dynamic can be overpowering.

I remember an ad that was run years ago showing a photograph of an obviously impatient purchasing manager sitting alone on a chair. He was looking into the camera, but the intent was to show that he was speaking to some "poor slob" of a salesman, who, if the purchasing manager had anything to do with it, had already lost the battle before the first shot had even been fired. Underneath the photo of him on the chair were a number of statements and one single leveling question at the close:

- I don't know who you are.
- I don't know your or your company's sales philosophy.
- I don't know what product or product line you are selling.
- I don't know the company you represent.
- I don't know if your product works or performs properly.
- I don't know what prices you are asking, but from the looks of you, they will be too high.
- I don't know why you are wasting my time.
- I don't plan on buying anything because I am very happy with my current supplier.
- I don't have more than five minutes for you.
- *Now, what was that you wanted to talk to me about?*

Talk to sales professionals. This kind of situation is not an over-dramatization. There is no substitute for the salesperson who can listen to this and then, in spite of an almost hopeless situation, start the courageous journey, visit by visit, up the hill to convince this kind of person to buy his product.

When asked how many salespersons they have in their organization, some senior executives will maintain that everyone having contact with a customer or a lead or an interested party is a salesperson. That's nice public relations language, and perhaps effective in a limited way to underline your and your organization's total commitment to sales, but how many of these people are directly dependent upon closing a sale for their income? The salesperson walking into the customer's office alone is the person carrying the real burden of the sales effort and no one else.

As CEO, you need to avoid attitudinal gridlock that could arise among your salespeople within your internal support organization. Beware the possible acrimony that exists among members of your sales team, the sales managers, and other company departments upon whom your salespeople depend for help and support. These areas might include product availability (Production), product reliability and zero failure performance (Quality Control), newness and unique value propositions (New Product Development), pull marketing (Marketing and Public Relations), correct and timely credit and debit bookings (Finance Department), prompt delivery of required product (Purchasing, Production, and Shipping), and quick turnaround solution of problems (Customer Service Department). In their occasional frustration with sales force loop de loops, the personnel of these departments often do not pay enough attention to who is really paying the bills in the company: the customer. There can even be times when one manager, either consciously or unconsciously, will organize a little payback through a particularly difficult salesman or sales division. Such a manager, just doing his job by the numbers instead of recognizing the need for focused urgency and quick solutions, can be enough to foul up the best sales intentions of a company. In countering this kind of problem, you need to do two things: continuously monitor your company to ensure that the communication and coordination between the various responsible departments consistently function in the proper fashion, and, at set periods, meet personally with all of the relevant department managers to go through any possible impediments, real or perceived, that stand in the way of their supporting your sales group. Your sales management team should be represented at such meetings.

Be sure your sales managers are not between a rock and a hard place. Sales managers are responsible for hiring, training, motivating and leading the sales team and, with them, producing the numbers anchored in the company budget. Thus, when sales levels fluctuate, it may be difficult for those managers to explain to management why the up or down took place in a specific week or month. Their frustration is also often due to the fact that only a minimum of sales metrics have been established to accurately measure the relative performance of each salesperson, territory, or division. The top management of too many companies doesn't see the value in putting major money behind an effective system of metrics so that its sales management team can really *lead*. The result is a fog of numbers and frustrated sales managers.

The whole company is dependent upon both the accuracy of the sales forecasts and the subsequent sales performance of the sales group. When sales fall below anticipated levels, or fluctuate wildly (particularly to the downside), frustration and even anger can build up, both in the sales force as well as in the overall company. Some of your salespeople may leave your company because they conclude it's easier to make sales elsewhere. Their leaving costs you sales and makes you partially blind in one of your territories. As a result of these changing circumstances, your purchasing people face an accumulation of useless inventories and the nightmares associated with that problem.

Sales professionals live in a world of facts, beliefs, assumptions, and hope. While they ostensibly know their markets, they are, generally speaking, not the best people to call upon for accurate sales forecasting. One of the planning mantras in many companies is "plan from the bottom up" and that means the salespeople are often right in the midst of any forecasting or budgeting exercise. As CEO, you must have additional ways and means to forecast properly and as accurately as possible.

No need to despair. There is quite a bit you *can* do to obtain better running-year forecasting efforts from your sales group. Forecasting accuracy is very clearly impacted by the professional quality and experience of your sales group. Consider these critical prerequisites for obtaining well considered sales forecasts *and* a top sales performance from your sales group:

- Verify that your salespeople are reliable observers of the market scene. To do this, create frequent opportunities to meet with groups of your salespeople to listen to their problems and discuss with them their views on the market and their customers' needs. You might also consider creating a Customer Advisory Board, headed by your sales director, with which you can consult concerning the market and the direction it might take going forward. Their opinions will be pungent, to the point, and helpful in your forecasting effort.

- Be sure your sales territories are well-balanced in terms of market, travel time, and sales potential (new customer acquisition and existing customer maintenance). This gives your salespeople more face time with the customers, creating a better-informed sales force.

- Confirm or work toward ensuring that salesperson fluctuation is low or non-existent.

- Have well-designed and appropriate sales performance metrics (accountability) that will provide detailed and transparent information on individual and distribution channel customer purchase performance, as well as trends in that performance.

- Continually check or work toward ensuring that customer purchases and margins achieved with those customers are at or near the highest possible benchmark budget levels set by your sales group and approved by you. Implicit in this performance is this: If they produce high-quality numbers, then you can assume they know their customers well, are managing them effectively, and therefore can better estimate what those customers can or will do in the future. These are the salespeople who can tell you what their customers' weekly sell-through is. By knowing this number and their customers' current inventory levels, they can make a very good judgment call on when the next orders will come and what they will consist of. From there, it is a short walk for your salespeople to a sound forecast and fulfillment of budget.

- Have an appropriate and fair compensation system to reward individual sales performance on a monthly, quarterly, and annual basis. Get your top performers in front of you, and involve them in discussions on the direction of your business and sales volume.

- Get your sales managers away from their offices. Their job is to spend most of their time out in the field leading and working with your salespeople, both creating and maintaining sales momentum. Also, have your purchasing people travel in the field with your top salespeople several times a year. Ditto for Customer Relations management.

- Have a benefits-oriented marketing effort to the end-user. Your salespeople must understand that it is not their opinion that counts in convincing the customer, but the value put upon the product by the prospective customer himself.

- Establish consensus among your sales professionals that the company philosophy, business model, and the way in which the company conducts itself represent the key decision factors in buying—even more than the products/services or their features themselves. An honorable approach like this wins hearts and minds.

You are thinking: I want exactly this kind of a top sales organization. I want to eliminate as much of the frustration and emotions in my company's sales activities as I can. I want to see accurate and substantive forecasting performances.

Time to stop imagining and instead, reflect carefully on the problems or obstacles you may encounter when you set out to create that first-class sales organization:

- **Perfect Hires.** If ever an imperfect world existed, then the world of the sales group, its constitution, its work ethic, and its mode of operation embody that definition. There will seldom be the "perfect 10" hire of a new salesperson because you can't look behind the forehead of the person with whom you are dealing.

- **Manager/Sales Confusion.** A good sales professional will generally not make a good sales manager. Good sales pros are hunters; they live for the reward of the close. Managers hunt numbers: They live (or should live) for budgets and for meeting sales targets. There are exceptions to this rule, but don't assume that the exception is sitting in front of you.

- **The 3-5-2 rule.** Just as there is a numerical relationship that describes your sales and customer relationship (20 percent of your customers will generally give you 80 percent of your sales), there is also a similar measure that describes the "competence content" of your sales force.

  — For any 10 people in your sales group, the **first group,** (two to three people) will generally be the stars, proud of their profession and going the extra mile every day. These are the highly ambitious and qualified salespeople in your organization with whom you experience nothing but pleasure when meeting with them, traveling with them to customers, and paying them bonuses. You look at them and ask, "Where are the cloning experts?"

— The **middle group** will contain five to six members. These are your standard and reliable performers. They are the faces you will see over and over again at sales meetings, all loyal, hardworking, and dependable.

— The **third group** usually contains one to two members. These people are the ones who are more or less along for the ride. Many of these kinds of salespeople have done the "tour," meaning they have worked here and there for other companies in the same industry, and perhaps in the same product area your company is involved in. This is just one more ride on the carousel for them. In summary, this rule essentially says that you have lost or are losing between 10 and 20 percent of the effectiveness of the dollars you are spending on your sales organization. Do you like these numbers?

• **It's all about the money.** You know that many in the company think that sale force organizations are expensive (and inefficient) propositions; in fact, sales sometimes represents the largest single expense position in the overall operating budget of a company. Accountability for the amount of money being invested in sales is part of your responsibility. The amount going out must fit the performance coming in and *vice versa*. If sales lag and yet your salespeople are off to a far away place to celebrate last year's sales achievements, you shouldn't place a bet on how fast you are going to be receiving major flak inside the company. If your salespeople have high fixed incomes and relatively little variable income—and the latter is based on a couple of loose performance metrics which never really count—then you should take a minute to consider what people in your organization, as well as your board, think about your leadership and the way you manage the company's investment in sales.

• **Short-versus long-term sales group responsibilities.** Companies don't grow and prosper because they get immediate or quarterly gratification through good short-term sales group performance. Investments in this area are just that: significant sums of money that are being invested over the long term in building a sales-competent group that can produce both quantity and quality in its group results. There are no short cuts, no quick fixes, or cheap ways to reach this objective.

As CEO of your company, top sales performance, both for the short but also long term, is what you want. Carefully selected personnel, competent leadership, a morally responsible customer service department, and an all-pervasive orientation to continuing growth in quality sales revenue are the must-haves for achieving this goal. Put real grit and substance into the way your sales groups take care of business.

Hiring Those Who Are Born to Sell

First of all, let's look at what you need to do to dramatically increase the percentage of good candidates interviewing with your company for sales jobs. These recruiting methods may not always be the nicest, but you certainly know by now that business is not a polite croquette game played on a neat lawn.

In every territory where you are still looking to hire or have had problems with past hires, visit your most loyal customers, or have your sales management team do so. Ask these customers to give you names of sales professionals who have a good reputation in that territory and in the industry. Who is it that they and their colleagues trust and respect? Which of the competitor's salespersons do your customers smile at when those people walk into their office? Make a list of these people and then have one of your people in the adjoining territory or one of your sales managers call these people and meet them. Your goal is to recruit them.

If you and your sales management team visit an industry trade show, carefully observe the performance of other companies' salespeople going on about their jobs. One of them, perhaps a good one, might even be talking to you and telling you about his products—in a way you wish he were talking about yours. Get his business card and proceed from there.

Constantly observe your younger potential management talent in the various internal operations of your company. Work with your HR Department on this project. Be on the lookout for young and ambitious men and women who are already on the fast track in their current non-sales positions. Challenge them to spend a year or two in sales, to test and prove their ability to produce tangible and visible results. By doing so, they will promote their careers in a most effective manner.

Maintain positive contacts with other vendors serving your customers. Encourage your sales people and directors to do the same. In the ebb and flow of business within your industry, a non-competitor company may hit a rough spot and have to eliminate people and territories. If you have prepared the ground well, that company, wanting to soften the blow of the downsizing among those affected, might want to talk to you about the possibilities of employment with *your* company for several of those affected individuals. The sales director of a major company in our industry once told me that, even though it was not his direct responsibility, he had traveled more than 1,000 miles to explain to a particular salesperson personally why it was necessary to cut his employment short. The sales manager obviously thought highly of this person and recommended him to me. We hired him. This is an excellent, though rare, source of candidates.

Finally, practice a continual and rigorous application of your unique as well as standard search and recruiting methods. With the involvement of your HR Department, you will also locate a number of interesting candidates from whom you can choose. As standard procedure, your HR Department and your sales management should maintain contact with candidates who occasionally write to your company asking about sales jobs. There's also no harm in having your sales managers meet and talk with such people, even though there may be no immediate need for them.

Putting Your Company's Mission Statement Into the Sales Equation

As discussed earlier, one of your major priorities is to ensure that your salespeople understand and can sell what your company is and what and why it exists. In addition to that model and its relevance for your customers, you must also make sure to connect your salespeople to the *core values* of your company. That requires business philosophy training. Even good salespeople often make one of the classic mistakes in sales: They jump immediately into the product/price/terms side of the equation in the first five minutes of a customer meeting. They do this, perhaps understandably, with existing customers, but they also very often do this, which is not so understandable, with potential new customers.

There is a simple reason to discuss values and mission statement first, and product afterwards. The *serious* purchasing manager will have several non-product related issues in his mind that will interest him more than immediately knowing what kind of an introductory deal he is going to get. The serious buyer is not really interested in or worried about the relationship with you during the good times. He will want to know how your company will behave toward his business when seemingly unsolvable problems arise. He will ask himself how your company will conduct itself when it has to balance its own business needs against those of its customers. And he will want straight and verifiable answers to that question, ongoing proof that your company doesn't just talk a good value game. Your sales team has to be equipped to articulate and continually sell the vital connection between your company's core values and the people for whom these values exist—among them, your customers.

Some purchasing managers are out for the short-term, of course, and won't even give you the time of day for this discussion. You and your sales team are not going to be able to change him or his company's approach to your products or services. He will buy as he sees fit. But for the other serious people in the industry, the core values of your company, and their uniform and consistent application to the customer relationship are what count in a successful sales partnership.

The Moral Component of Customer Relations in Your Mission Statement

While your salespeople are out selling, some of the bridges they crossed in making the sale may already be on fire behind them. Every customer knows there are going to be errors and issues in any customer/company relationship, and they cost both you and your customer money. The dollar amount may be small, but those issues can also have a more serious and longer-lasting cost for your customer, namely, possible substantial loss of reputation and perhaps loss of their own customers due to your company's mistakes.

How do you reduce not only the short-term monetary fallout, but also the potential long-term permanent fallout, including customer loss, in such a situation? You prepare for such events happening *long in advance*.

Ensure that all personnel involved either directly or indirectly with your customers have not only understood the importance of the core values of your company, but also practice them daily in their work with your customers. They must understand that when your company sells a product or a service, your company takes on a moral responsibility for the reliable performance of that product. Some CEOs would call this good business practice. It is, but it is good business practice with an "attitudinal extra" that makes the difference between good customer relations and an extraordinary selling and buying relationship with your customers. To illustrate this, assume that you discover that there is potentially a technical problem with a small number (less than 1 percent) of parts in a shipment you have just sent your customer for their scheduled production. Immediately, you need to provide him with a warning. Explanations alone are not adequate. But first send a truck with replacements, no questions asked, before you even initiate your warning call to the customer. In a second example, your purchasing department has indicated that there could possibly be a delay in your company receiving a particular component necessary to produce a specific part destined for one of your customers. Don't wait and see—act. Warn your customer immediately so that he can make adjustments in his production scheduling or shipment plans. If your customer decides that *he* would like to wait and see, then you can accept that. Your moral responsibility toward this customer has been fulfilled.

In a third scenario, assume that your company has caused a major problem in your customer's business. One of the most effective means to show that your company takes that problem seriously, as well as to neutralize any negative behavior on the part of that customer would involve you and the responsible salesperson visiting the customer. Many customers don't expect a CEO to be involved in such daily issues. By visiting that customer, you will show that you are earnest and personally committed to resolving the problem promptly. Don't think that your customers (and your own people) won't talk postively about your visit and the help you gave them when they meet with colleagues around the industry.

In conducting your customer relations business in this fashion, you foster goodwill and build a reservoir of trust.

The ancillary benefit of your company's recognition of the importance of moral responsibility and of living that core value lies in the fact that your company will be able to build up a series of goodwill "plus points" with your customers. The existence of this cushion of goodwill serve you well should other more serious customer-related problems occur in the future. Your customer is unlikely to overreact or even consider ceasing doing business with your company. He will have experienced, during the course of his ongoing business relationship with your company, a consistent pattern of your company caring about his business, and remember that when something unpleasant occurs.

Designing Sales Team Remuneration

When setting up the *variable* part of your income plan for the sales organization, design it to provide three kinds of payments: performance related monthly payments, quarterly payments, and annual payments. Each payment accomplishes a specific goal: The monthly commissions relate to sales unit or sales revenue performance achieved during the running month, the quarterly commissions are keyed to several major strategic sales objectives of the company during the year, and annual commissions or bonuses are keyed to securing the overall performance of the company in the running year and prepping it for the next budget year.

Salespeople enjoy this steady stream of payments over the whole year time period. First of all, it gives them the immediate reward they seek. Prompt financial acknowledgement of what they've accomplished triggers positive emotions about repeating that performance again. The concept also very neatly focuses your salespeople's consistent attention over the whole year on those different goals for which they carry primary responsibility. And it requires them to manage in a timely and effective manner their efforts tied to reaching these respective period goals.

Achieving Effective Sales Management

For your sales managers, "management" often means "office," so they spend considerable time there. But good sales managers do *not* spend most of their time in the office; they are out in the field, helping their team, either directly or indirectly, to make their numbers, and to realize the optimum sales potential for the company. Good sales managers have a mental video of their major customers' offices and their operations because they know and work with those customers. Don't accept less than this kind of engagement whatever the supposed administrative burden may be. Work to minimize this burden and get those people out into the field.

In sales management, "sales controlling" is a phrase sometimes used to describe the metrics of sales management. It is a misnomer with a negative touch. At the finance and department level, "controlling" is an apt description for what goes on. You don't have to use the same word with salespeople who generally are sensitive about other people breathing down their necks about performance, though. Controlling is a necessary function, but not a motivating word.

In performance-based sales management, it is of particular importance to give special attention to the following two metrics.

New Customer Acquisition and Mid-Term Performance Accountability

Look closely at any company's sales growth aspirations and you will most likely see the need to broaden and strengthen the buying customer base. In most companies, when new customers are acquired, these new customers remain in the new category only for the year in which they "join" the company. In the following year, your new customer yearlings will disappear into the overall standard customer database and no longer be a *separate* category, subject to a separate performance-based analysis of their ongoing contribution to the company's sales progress. Your goal should be to put yourself in a position, using appropriate metrics and benchmarks, to judge your sales group's performance (individually and collectively) in finding and retaining high-quality new customers. Without this kind of information, you have no ability to confirm if your new customers have become an effective part of the stronger customer base you intend to build for your company.

Furthermore, what you *have* effectively done is release your salespeople from any future obligation to work specifically with these new customers and build them into long-term buying customers. Some of your salespeople may do so because they know the value of their new customers, having fought hard and long to win them. They will want to earn commissions on them. But most of your salespeople will be thinking along the lines of immediate results: The company wants a certain number of new customers, and here they are. Remember the old statement: If it doesn't get measured or nobody is looking, it generally will not get done.

These new customers have cost your company an enormous amount of time, money, and people resources. Frequent and repeated visits went into closing the first sale. You know that new customer acquisition is important for the quantitative and qualitative *growth* of your customer base. They represent the nascent part of your future revenue base. It is important, therefore, that you have your company follow new customer development during a period of *at least three years.* This would involve your company establishing comparative individual new customer performance data stretching over the respective three year periods. Here are the important components of those metrics:

- Number of total new customers acquired in initial year, compared to new customers remaining at the end of the second and third year.
- Average total sales per customer, as well as individual unit or service revenues per year.
- Percentage of new customer sales using three-year comparison to overall company sales during same time period (broken down by region/territory).
- Average new customer order size, and frequency of ordering per year.
- Average individual unit product or service contribution margins per year as well as the cumulative total margin effect from all customers.
- Percentage of total company product line or services by new customers, both individually and collectively.
- Rankings of territories by their respective benchmark performances in all of these categories.

Using this methodology, you will be able to clearly see how successful your sales group has been in building your customer base. In addition, you will know how many of the new customers that they acquired in a specific year are left after three years. You will also know what these customers have contributed in sales and margin to the overall company performance during this period of time.

There is one more issue you should take into consideration when thinking about a new customer. Determine why a certain number of your new customers buy sporadically, or have ordered only once since coming on board as new customers. In order to improve your acquisition efforts constantly, as well as the management of those new customers during the critical three-year period, you need to know what caused these customers to not order any more of your product. Also look for reasons in the non-sales disciplines of your company, such as new product, shipping, or marketing. You should know *every one* of the reasons why the company investment has been undermined, or has not brought the required results.

Reactivation of Your Existing Customers in the First Quarter of the Year

Your company customer lists and your active customer lists are definitely not the same. Generally, it is not difficult to guess which one of the lists has the lower number of customer names on it. Do you really know how many and how often your customers come back to buy from you and how many do not? And, of particular importance, do you know whether the comeback rate in the critical first quarter of your current business year is better or worse than the rate you had the previous year in the same period?

Competition in the market is increasingly a matter of fierce firefights. Promotions, contests, special terms and conditions, unit rebates. This kind of fierce competitive activity is particularly prevalent during the first three to six months of any running budget year. One can therefore assume that you will have a very detailed marketing and promotion program, aimed, among other things, at keeping your customers continually coming back for more. But you will also need complete and reliable numerical information to make clear what customers actually are doing in the first critical months of any new year. Have they ordered since the beginning of the year? How much and how frequently have they ordered compared to what they did in the first quarter of last year? Are the investments that you have recently made in personnel and marketing producing the desired results? Here are the most important metrics you will need to analyze your customer activity rate in the critical first quarter:

- A list of last year's buying and paying customers, ranked by sales, territory, and region.
- A month-by-month reporting in the new budget year on the number and the percentage of old-year customers active again by territory and region, and those territory and regional rankings by performance.
- Number of orders placed by reactivated customers compared to the previous year, as well as average order size comparisons month-to-month and year-to-year. You can run a report on this starting with those customers who have ordered and/or reordered the most and then let it run down to those customers who have not ordered at all.
- Undertake a similar analysis of your Top 50 Customer List. Every single one of your top 50 customers should be active and exceeding last year's first quarter numbers by the end of the first quarter of the current year.

Your goal: Achieve a more forceful and sales-effective start in the new budget year compared to the previous year. What you don't want to happen is for you to get to your April or May end-of-the-month numbers, see that they are bad, and then have to ask yourself, "What happened?"

FAST-TRACKING NEW PRODUCTS: EATING DUST IS BAD NUTRITION

You and your company slide into irrelevance if you do not anticipate and service existing and possible future market needs. You must be prepared to act fast in response to shifts in demand for your products and/or services, and be prepared to use appropriate company resources to create demand for totally new, unique, and market-oriented products currently not in the market. The alternative: Your company might survive (you won't), but it won't grow.

When discussing the relative importance of corporate facts of life, practically everyone would agree that company personnel, and their training, experience, motivation, focus, quality of work, morale, and integrity affect the fortunes of a company. Sound finances make your operational plans possible; a realistic business model and innovative user-oriented product being sold in the market contribute to your chances of success. "The market" is people, companies, or other user categories, so that means you want to consistently and continually offer products or services that such target groups consider applicable to *their* wants and needs. Above all, your company should be structured to deliver this kind of customer-oriented performance on a priority basis.

New product/service is the engine that drives your company's growth. When tuned properly, it will produce solid short-term results, fuel long-term company strength, enhance your company's reputation and support, and grow company value. It will also put you where you want to be: well ahead of the competition. Conversely, if you are forced to eat your competitors' dust, you have your company involved in a very bad form of business nutrition.

This can't just be any new product thrown into the market, of course. These are choices you will want to avoid: choosing a product because it looks good, just does the job, is cheap to produce, or you were able to pick it up through a discounted license deal. If, however, you really want to play the game successfully in the market, then you must *continually* think in terms of unique and market-oriented new product. If that is your intention and purpose, then here is a checklist of the most important criteria for judging the suitability and market-appropriateness of that product. The product must:

- Fit the overall corporate strategy of the company. It must result from the company using every creative and innovative strength it possesses to the fullest extent.

- Be founded upon a competent, detailed, and no-holds barred analysis and judgment of the short-, middle-, and long-term attractiveness and marketability of the product and its value proposition for the *user*. Nothing else counts; don't even think about looking for an alternative to this.

- Please the eye with its design, color, and general design lines. There is no doubt that senses play a major role in forming a purchase decision. People have to like how the product looks, feels, or smells. In a metaphorical way, this applies to services as well. Your service has to have an attractive "look and feel," which is often related to the people who provide the service. These are the kind of people you generally want to have around you. The same applies to Web-based services, which should have navigational and visual appeal, and simplicity to help form the positive perception that affects a purchasing decision.

- Be one that dares to challenge the established standards of the product group in the industry or a service that underlines your company's commitment to user-friendly concepts in a unique way.

- Originate within a corporate structure that is not bogged down with layers of hierarchy, and perhaps dominated by product managers with big egos and even bigger, unrealistic sales dreams. Your respective development groups should be positioned so they are, at the most, two or three layers removed from you. Your job is to be involved in critically assessing every new product, staying informed about its progress through the development process, and getting a respectful, but accurate, reading on your people's egos versus the real world, in the judgment of any new product's chances at market success. Your development people need to hear from you personally if they are doing a good job.

- Have had the benefit of production, marketing, sales, and purchasing staff participating together as one group from the beginning of the development phase. If they perform in isolation, the first price you will pay will be in the form of delays and wasted time caused by an almost total lack of communication between the appropriate departments. This lack of integrated planning will lead to only one thing: You will have compromised the project and its financial viability right at the start. Consequently, don't be surprised by the excessive development cost overruns you will face later. The second price, and this is the big one, will be in not even getting close to the target price necessary to create substantial market interest and generate the required unit sales and margin volume. Finally, when the product starts rolling out of the factory, your company could potentially incur higher production costs because of a lack of or loss of production efficiencies due to the product's possibly overly complex design. If you get in between the working ends of these negative scissor effects, you have probably already lost any market advantage you may have had before your product has even reached the marketplace.

- Not represent a one-off product development excursion with your company putting just one single product into the market. If you want to go to market with a new product, then make certain it will be part of a balanced product line containing different product price points from low- to high-end. If your marketing strategy calls for only all high-end or only all low-priced market entry level products, then the goal of a balanced and complete product line must be met within one or the other of these respective market price segments. Eventual product line extensions are totally separate issues. They consist of further product additions after your initial line has been developed and successfully established in the market.

- Not entail an attempt by management to move up-market when the whole image and reputation of the company has been built upon low-end, price-aggressive product. However, if the company has positioned itself at the high end of the price/quality equation, then it is perfectly legitimate to tuck a lower-priced product or product line underneath the existing high-end quality product. This umbrella effect, based upon the company's up-market image and reputation, will help to ease the new line into the market and give it almost immediate legitimacy in the relevant trade/distribution channels.

- Have the competition playing catch up. You cannot even think of calling yourself and your company unique and innovative if you don't set out to scare your competition every time with a new product that leaves them behind in the market, eating *your* dust. At some point in time, they will have to come up with something, too, but you know that will take time. And you are already on to the next mountain top with no dust in sight.

- Reflect thoroughly vetted component sourcing if the product requires purchasing outside of the company. A critical part of product development is vendor production of prototypes and their testing and approval in company laboratories or facilities. To avoid delays, frustration, communication difficulties, and missed market opportunity, you must have your *own* company personnel installed *for the duration* in the vicinity of those vendors, working with them to produce the required prototypes of the product or component in a timely fashion. Only then will you have the guarantee that your specific product component requirements, tolerances, composition, and performance, will be in that prototype when it leaves the vendor's shop bound for further tests in your company facilities. Otherwise, you will be involved in the month- or year-long game called "bounce the prototype back and forth." Mistakes will occur, the prototypes will often not match the required product specifications, and the necessary communication will not function optimally. Other results are delays, frustration, and possibly missing the market with a product that, at its design conception, was right on.

- Have been tested both officially and in practice. For example, just getting a product certification from Underwriter's Laboratory (UL) isn't adequate enough. Stringent testing of the product(s) under real-use market conditions is. Do not put a product into the market and get a reputation among your distribution channels for "testing" product by selling it into the market too early, thereby forcing your customers to carry the brunt of the initial problems and technical faults that will almost always arise.

- Have gone through the zero-series production stage and then been moved on, under stringent quality control benchmarks, to full production. That gives you the ability to provide adequate product quantities for the initial pipelining of your new product(s), and enough for immediate follow-up orders to the market. Careful with trying to use product supply delays to "hot up" initial orders for a product. Your dealers will thank you for not doing it. They will remember this as a positive gesture to them. At some later time, they will most likely reward you by buying other product from your existing product line when you want to put some extra "standard" product out for sale in their stores or warehouses.

- Hit the 100-percent mark in your quality-control standards in the demo phase. From A to Z, be sure the product you set aside for market demo purposes works *flawlessly* before sending it to *any* customer. If the product requires technical aid or user training for it to function optimally, then send your best sales engineer with it when it goes to your selected advance customers.

- Be fairly and competitively priced with appropriate terms and conditions and exciting promotional and launch backup as well as follow-up promotional efforts at appropriate time after launch marks.

- Gives your salespeople the exciting opportunity to be up and running to get to their customers with the new product. You will have this kind of reaction from your sales people only if they have a product in their hands where no excuses about value proposition, price/value relationship, and user advantages are necessary and where the customer says, "Wow, you guys have really been listening to us." Otherwise, all your salespeople will have to offer is a difficult or embarrassing explanation as to why the product isn't exactly what the market would like to see and buy.

- Not be announced or shown over and over again at trade shows and in the media and then not appear in the market until much later. If your company record in this regard involved announcing that a new product will be available in six months, knowing all the while that your company has never held to that time period, then you are deluding yourself and your customers. The idea of showing product in the gestation stage at trade shows is patently dangerous. Your competitors will be smiling, but your customers won't.

- Be so conceived and developed that it won't take critical hit after hit when the media or competent product critics from the industry get their hands on the product and conduct their tests. Analysts and reviewers seem to know more about product potential and usefulness than many manufacturers and designers. For example, how astounding is it that car manufacturers introduce and promote 20 to 30 new models every year to the market—and this after several or more years of development, consumer research, and testing—only to read subsequently in the press how miserably they have failed to bring to their markets a top-quality and consumer-oriented product?

- Have all of your people, upon leaving the auditorium after the new product presentation, excitedly talking about the amazing new on-target product and not the really good jelly doughnuts that were served. What do you think your sales will look like after *that* kind of reaction? "On target" means your company knows what fast, focused, and consequent mean in the development of new product. On target means that your company is culturally and organizationally set up to create and bring to market a whole series of winners. It also means *you personally* are on target.

Do not allow the corporate shuffle, that state of affairs described as "can't get anything done because nobody listens or comes across with what we need," to get in the way of what you and your creative people should have in order to keep the company and new product development moving forward. Your company will not be successful if you as CEO always operate under the assumption that your development and marketing people are taking care of "things." While you may have a top New Product Development department with a top manager heading it up, you personally must take care of the shop as well. Talk and walk the new product conspicuously and continually. While there will hopefully be many times when you can celebrate your leadership in bringing such unique and successful product or services to the market, be careful. There is one potentially negative factor that can sneak its way into every well-intentioned new product development cycle. It involves the conflict between the required time-to-market factor and the over-development syndrome. Too often, with competitive pressures and the need to push growth, companies in the early stage of the development process will not clearly establish the timeframe within which the new product *must* be made market-ready and then launched. What often gets in the way of completion of a particular product's development is an interesting thought process that goes something like this: "We've found a new feature we like for the product and we think we should add it." If you in fact have something really new and different in the making, beware of the ravages of time, during which you repeatedly fall in love with all the great things one can still do with the product to make it really "hot." What started out looking as though it would be 150-percent a winner could rapidly deteriorate into an also-ran.

Ask yourself these questions:

- Have you fallen so in love with the technical development of the product and how proud you will be to present something unique that you are constantly improving that product?
- Could that product you are looking at already be the fifth generation in your new product development cycle and yet it is still under development?
- Have you forgotten what your little boy told you when you spoke to him about how great home runs were at a baseball game and he looked at you and said, "A lot of well-hit singles in a row—and at the right time—will win the game, too, dad." Simpler first generation solutions present many attractive possibilities when you are trying to maintain momentum in your company's growth.
- Is it possible that the initial conception of the new product was so off-base in terms of price and features that you are having to spend more development time making up for the fact that the product was actually a non-starter when it came out of the "creative box?"

While ensuring that you have your new product development set up correctly, don't worry if *not* every product development activity is oriented to maximizing your company growth and prosperity. A few esoteric or experimental things in the making may be and should be part of your overall new product development activity. Nothing wrong with that, but they can take time to develop. So equip your current growth plans with market-oriented, unique mainstream product. Get it out there into the market in a *timely* fashion and then move on to your second- and third-generation product development.

New market-oriented products or services are *the* key to driving your growth and your success in the market. Add to that dynamic the sales and marketing qualities of a top sales group and you have a potent combination that will, without a doubt, forcefully drive your sales momentum and support the growth in value of your company.

Key Priorities

- To get the optimum sales performance out of your company, you must understand and have an appreciation for not only the performance potential of your sales group, but also for its limitations. If you haven't spent time in sales, then pay special attention to the attitudinal and unique characteristics of the sales function and how that function can be your friend or your enemy.

- Your competition is not sitting in its offices designing the shape of a white flag they will use in surrendering. Two of the most important words driving the growth of your company are *new* and *improved*. Don't assume that your top product development people will handle the situation and thereby always do the positive market-oriented thing. Get the keys and drive that car personally.

- Top sales performance must be defined and it must be measured. That performance depends almost wholly on the quality of the people you send out to confront your competition in the market. Building a strong sales group is not just a matter left to chance. Know exactly what you want and how to get it when considering how you intend to recruit, train, and measure your salespeople.

Chapter 3

*Y*OU ARE THE IN-HOUSE VALUE PROPOSITION

You may think that everything is a team effort, and that management consensus on key tactical and strategic issues is the only way to move your company forward. The fact of the matter is that you have a title with the initials CEO. Don't sell yourself short. The conductor leading the orchestra doesn't play an instrument during the concert but, without him up front, the music being produced may contain discord and off-key notes. Your influence and ability count. Take the pat on the head you have earned getting to where you are. Now show what you can really do.

WHO IS REALLY RUNNING THE PLACE, YOU OR EVERYONE ELSE?

The answer begins with the usual suspects: board; shareholders or investors; several of their cronies who are pulling or pushing for certain things to happen; key management; the market; your top customers increasingly throwing their weight around; competitors;

lawmakers and regulators; bankers with their zero-risk approach; your CFO with her conservative approach to everything; your dealer board that is demanding changes in company policy relating to distribution channels and the apparent favoritism of one channel over another; your production head rejecting the last production planning change because there have been too many of them in the past several months; your product development people who have informed you they are sorry about your time schedule and the advertising is already bought, but the new product is going to be three months late; your lawyers, who don't want you to talk and are checking everything you write for public consumption down to the last comma; one or two management fiefdoms with uncrowned chieftains who are surreptitiously making decisions without consulting you; one or two of your internal competitors currently thinking they can do the job better than you can.

Are these the people running the place? Where has your power gone if you are constantly being buffeted by problems, issues, drama, or blockades instigated by people, most of whom have less official power than you? Have you lost it? Is your next step abdication?

Not in your dreams.

This is a typical picture of what you face every day as the CEO. Your power has not gone anywhere. You are trusted by the board; the market thinks you are the best thing that has happened to the company in the last 10 years. And you still sit at the working end of the conference table in the correct chair. What you are experiencing is standard flak and standard daily disturbances. This is where the power of your position and your ability to shape events and company direction must be brought directly into play. And the (sometimes intense) necessity to repeatedly do exactly that is not going to change.

Go one step further. What also will not change will be the occasional necessity to run directly over what is standing in your way. That is because there will be times when doing what you want to do corresponds exactly to what the company needs to and should be doing. And you are not going to ask anybody if you can do it or not, or if they would kindly change their minds and perhaps recognize that maybe your decision *is* the right step for the company. You step up and you do it.

The yelping and moaning that will sometimes take place afterwards are normal because there are not very many black or white alternatives in what you do when you want to lead your company successfully. Gray is typically the color of the day. You are there to make the tough calls, the marginal calls, the lose/win and win/lose calls—all of the hard decisions. That is what you are capable of doing and this is why you get paid the "big bucks."

At the same time, you are not going to run roughshod over everything and anything in the company just for the sake of exercising power. More often than not, your people have their reasons for doing or saying what they feel is correct or needed. You dialogue with them, and in most cases, everyone gets up afterwards, knowing a consensus and a way of proceeding have been agreed upon. you are the embodiment of cooperation 95 percent of the time. The other five percent? Ice water looks like it is boiling compared to the look on your face and the tone of your voice.

You know your real constituents are the stakeholders who are represented by the board. But the board has given you the title and, with it, the power, not only to do the easy things, but also to make the tough calls. You like consensus and teamwork? That is your goal, but it is not able to be practiced all the time.

You have certainly heard the statement: "Business is war." It is in the sense that practically everything will, at some time or another, require a fight or intense discussion. Every single one of those people and groups mentioned at the beginning of this chapter is watching you to see if you, when absolutely necessary, will fully exercise the power you have, step up and make the uncomfortable calls, and if you want to assert your stature unequivocally, put on that jacket with those four big letters, B-O-S-S. You won't want to do this every day, every week, or every month. Nevertheless, you know an occasional thin-lipped performance on your part doesn't hurt every once in a while.

Roll out the five percent and take care of what needs to be taken care of.

WORK YOUR STRENGTHS FOR ALL THEY ARE WORTH

You have advanced your career through astute leadership, sound ideas, reliability, good results, perhaps a mentor or two, your personality, and good judgment. To that you added persistence and passion in achieving the goals you set for yourself or those the company set down for you. You also like people, consider them to be anything but machines, and show these qualities in your daily work with them.

But sitting there thinking about all of this, you know full well that one of the major contributors to your success was an extraordinary and highly visible talent you have in a particular discipline or set of disciplines. It was that talent that had a direct impact on the operational success of your division or the company as a whole. And everybody who had anything to do with you or observed you on a daily basis knew it, too.

If you had spent most of your career in sales, loved the give and take of a deal, the rush of the close, admiration of your colleagues, and thankfulness of your customers for products and services reliably delivered, then that was a talent you used to the fullest extent in advancing your career. And your contribution as salesperson or a member of sales management was a major factor in driving the growth of your company's sales and profits.

Or perhaps you determined early on that your talents lay more on the technical side. This would have taken you into production, say in robotic systems design in manufacturing, or into product development where your talent in designing product with unique value propositions would have driven the company's growth, and your career, forward.

Or maybe you had a head and passion for numbers. Whatever set of extraordinary talents drove your career, you find yourself now as CEO in a position where you will be drawing upon both these talents as well as those you have acquired during your climb up the ladder in working within other operational disciplines of the company. The breadth and depth of knowledge will serve you well in those diverse responsibilities that fill your days.

Occasionally, however, you might find yourself thinking back to those days when you were almost totally immersed in that part of operations you really loved. You will remember the excitement and the impact you were able to make in your particular discipline.

Due to your organizational talent, those positions are now filled by top people. You can say proudly that the right people are in the right jobs working toward the right goals. Nevertheless, the memory and rewards of working with and using your talents in the trenches are still very real to you and the climb to the top using those talents was a great ride.

Going forward, you sense the urge—and may also see a reason—to get more intensely involved in contributing in those areas where you are still are at home, and to put extra effort into solving your company's problems in that area. What is the most effective way to go about doing this? What does your board expect of you? A typical expectation is that you become a strong generalist in your company and in your particular industry, lead the organization strategically, and grow the value of the company. Unquestionably, these job requirements are and will always remain your primary focus. But the question still stands: How can you structure your job so that it is also possible for you to make a contribution in those disciplines where your talents were once so relevant? In answering it, recall two of the most important characteristics of a successful CEO:

1. You know exactly *what questions must be asked* when the company is faced with finding a solution to a particular issue within *any* particular discipline. And this is particularly the case where you are, talent- and experience-wise, at home.

2. Based upon your experience, and having seen many similar types of issues in your past positions within that discipline, you are able to judge accurately the *quality and accuracy* of the suggestions or proposed solutions or judgments given to you in answer to these questions.

This way of proceeding is definitely the appropriate avenue you can take to quiet your yearning for action in your old discipline. As CEO, you are, first of all, already *automatically* involved in each and every one of the disciplines and operational units of your company. More to the point, you are involved in those where your talents and experience will be particularly appreciated and where they can be utilized for the good of the company.

Let's examine what the question means in daily practice and what the risks and rewards are.

First of all, you are not going to push the current management aside so that you can illustrate that your old brilliance in that discipline is still intact. Nor are you going to walk in unannounced to a meeting, or show up constantly in those company areas for which you have a particular affection. Nor are you going to second-guess from afar what is being decided in those respective

departments. Each of those actions is just a one-way ticket to creating frustration, anxiety, and friction between you and the people responsible for those
particular disciplines.

The best and most effective way to bring yourself and your talents into
play for the good of the company is by utilizing them in formal meetings on
budgets, strategic planning sessions, divisional or product line reviews, or in
the introduction of new software systems within the company. Or, in a less
formal sense, you can offer to make yourself available to your management
team, should there be a situation where your specific talents and point of view
could be of use. No one will resent your presence if you handle your talents
diplomatically. No one will resent you for asking these types of questions in
formal meetings, or for critiquing the answers. No one will even resent you for
occasionally dropping by the department or the division to talk about matters
at hand. They want you to bring your smarts and your experience to bear on
their specific situations and to help them move past momentary difficulties.
Don't kid yourself: this may not be explicit in your job description; the board
will not require you to do it, but everyone will be looking to see that you, not
as Houdini, but as a talented individual, are able to continue to impact the
progress of the company with your specific talents. Your talents are part of
your aura and your standing, as well as part of the reason you have the job you
do. Being there for your people, posing the right questions, and judging the
answers and commenting on them *is* also a part of that job, because you are
an acknowledged expert with a track record to back it up.

One final and very important point: When you have made that contribution, and the results are in and show that the project has turned into a major
success, don't sit there and hint that all of the good things that happened
probably wouldn't have happened if you had not been directly involved. Be
satisfied that it has all worked out so well.

Let the full credit accrue to the person heading up the division, region,
or department. Let him or her, or the whole division, enjoy the spotlight and
rewards. It will result in quiet respect for you ("he's still got it!") within the
whole company, and loyalty on the part of those you helped and who know
how you contributed to building their position, image, and success within the
company.

DETAILS: THE LYNCH PINS OF YOUR SUCCESS

There are a lot of sayings around about details, some humorous, some serious. A favorite American one is, *don't confuse me with the details.* Another somewhat more arrogant management cliché is, *I leave the details to others.* The Germans get hellish about the whole thing: *der Teufel steckt im Detail* (the devil is in the details) or *mich interessiert nur die grosse Ligne* (I just pay attention to the big picture.). And the French tend sometimes to pooh-pooh everything (except exquisite food) relating to details with the following bons mots: *c'est uniquement un seul petit detail* (it's only one small detail), or *oui, oui, les petites choses* (loose translation, said with a bored voice: Yes, yes, the small things).

Only one small detail? Well, small, single details, more often than not, tend to have more importance than their actual size. They can be killers if they are ignored or forgotten in a contract, project, financial analysis, or product development. Offhandedness—or even arrogance—in the face of such "small stuff" is dangerous and shortsighted. Worse yet, it is a sign of business immaturity and not having a clue about the potential danger or critical importance of our "little friends."

An executive or manager who is not in a position to talk in a fluid fashion *and in detail* about a specific company issue or development, touching upon all of the issues, large or small, is not a smart executive. If they can help it, smart executives do not leave anything, large or small, to chance. They make themselves the in-house encyclopedia on major issues pertinent to the growth of the company.

In certain situations, details should not be the stars of the show, for example, at board meetings, major policy statements, or presentations concerning key changes in business model or acquisition strategy. For such occasions, they are included in all of the required documents, and and don't require special attention. However, in the day-to-day operation of the company, they belong—without exception—front and center along with everything else that is relevant for the project or program at hand.

As mentioned in the previous section, two of the major attributes of a successful executive are the ability to formulate and ask the right questions at the right time, and the ability to judge the quality of the answers to questions posed. In practically every discussion where these two strengths come into play, the content of the discussion often revolves around detail. These questions imply directly the importance and central role of detail. The smart executive, knowing the details, and thinking about them in a three-dimensional manner (what do they mean for all aspects of this project?) will be able to show talent, power, and ability by citing and being able to discuss—mostly from memory—the salient and substantial details of the project or issue currently under discussion. Numbers, facts, actions, reactions—none of this will bother the smart CEO. Instead, this individual will show a particular joy in being able to juggle all of the relevant facts and details at will, as well as know that, while doing so, *power is exercised* in a particularly effective manner.

As a leadership and analysis tool, details serve a useful purpose. I knew well the CEO of a major mail order company in Germany who embodied the detail-smart executive. First of all, he never lost sight of the strategic and tactical aspects of every issue. In addition, he had taught himself how to handle, and categorize for recall purposes, all the details involved in a particular issue. People appearing before him to present their budgets or business plans had furrowed brows because they knew their presentation wouldn't take longer than 10 minutes. As a corollary, something one would be happy about under normal circumstances, namely the shortness of the discussion, was in this case cause for alarm and a high degree of alertness.

This executive did not go cold into such presentations; he had read all of the material in advance, and studied what was going to be put up on the screen the next day. He went looking for the lynch pin details of the issue. He checked for those details which, if ignored, shoved aside, or not properly respected, could mean project or product failure, or cause the basic premises of the critical assumptions and critical success factors surrounding and supporting the project to fall apart. They were the details he wanted to see, those that held the whole thing together. He had them down cold.

What everybody knew was how this executive judged the quality of the work and the proposal, not so much on the general contents of the paper, or solely on the financial attachments or the management summary, or the conciseness of the language. No, he did things quite differently.

With four or five questions, he would zero in on a small number of lynch-pin details that he considered critical; these were foundation details normally found two or three layers below the main surface or body of the presentation. This meant that if the presentation were to go well, the presenting individual had to have mastered every building block of his presentation, as well as their respective plausibility, value, and correlation to one another. If the person being questioned shot back the answer to a question about a specific detail with conviction and without hesitation, and did so with the same mastery of detail another four or five times, the presentation was essentially over. The last question was usually reserved for determining the presenting person's judgment of possible project execution risks.

Our smart executive would then nod approvingly and move on to the next subject and the next person. He knew that all bases had been covered if the manager could answer the questions he posed. And if the results fit, then the whole package being presented had integrity and would be approved. Woe, however, to the manager who stammered and stuttered, and would then say, "Well, you're going to have to trust me on this, it's all taken care of."

The simple, yet multi-faceted, lesson is this: If you want to show that you know what you are talking about, then you have got to get deeply involved in the details of the matter. Does that take time? Yes. Is it boring sometimes? Yes. Will you run the risk of losing sight of the forest because you are playing around in the brush and get hit in the eyes with twigs and branches? Not necessarily. And certainly not if you're good and have found a way to love, work, and feel at home in both of these worlds: the big picture view and the world of the all-important details.

In handling details this way, you might occasionally be accused of micromanaging, nit-picking, or losing touch with the big picture. *Micromanagement and respect for detail are two entirely different matters.* In the former, you are worried that something could be forgotten in the project or program execution phase, so you are constantly and continually chasing after a security blanket; you must constantly hear from your people that everything is under control. Details are involved here as well, but your involvement with them does not enhance your power, it diminishes it. While you consider all of this, you might also want to take a closer look at your organization and your trust in it, as well as how you personally have performed in manning that organization.

On the other hand, a source of genuine power is knowledge of details, a healthy respect for them and their potential harmful nature if forgotten, their importance in fitting together a presentation or concept or model so that it is a whole, their use in leadership situations, and their ability to enhance the respect your people hold for you.

Many young people today, particularly those who have become accustomed to having the Internet as their fast-performing information slave, want to show that they have the qualities to lead through their allegiance to and overweighting of big–picture concepts. Details, detailed analysis, and mastery of the important killer details are either boring or something for someone else to worry about. They love the roar of the crowd as they blow through lower-level promotion after promotion.

Things were no different when I was younger. At a performance review with my boss at a well-known cosmetic firm in Germany, and based upon my performance, which had resulted in my receiving a promotion (bigger sales division), I was expecting accolades, a salary increase, smiles, chocolates, and a boost in my fair-haired boy status. The salary increase took place, but everything else did not.

Instead, during that hour, I got a stern lecture on the need to have and develop a greater love and respect for detail. His message was simple: to not make details the be-all and end-all of everything I did, but to recognize their relevance and usefulness in leadership, and practice of that leadership. No doubt, he had looked at me and found me wanting. A little too full of myself, I had consciously or unconsciously distanced myself somewhat from the guts and the detail of the business at hand; I had concluded I didn't need much of it for what I intended to do and become. I had done well, but as for the future? Well, I realized that my future depended on my listening to and digesting what he had told me. I never forgot that day and I never forgot the man who took my whole measure and found me wanting in an important and substantial part of any successful business persona: knowledge of and respect for details, no matter how small.

Instead of ignoring most details, you can look at details in another and different way: you can go to the other extreme. About nine months after the previous conversation took place, I was running not only one, but two sales divisions, the first in the city of Munich and its environs, and the second, to the west toward and beyond Stuttgart. Both had been in the bottom third of the divisional rankings, but were now doing very well. You can believe that I was watching the important details that were *directly relevant* for division success. One day, I was asked to take on the position of Group Director of Sales for the company's French subsidiary near Paris. Shortly before leaving, my successor came to me and complained that he had found what he termed certain holes in the reporting and controlling of the division performance. A day was missing here or there. And some expense reports seemed to be arriving later than required. Yes, I confirmed to him, very possible.

He didn't let go. He stated that the comments in some of the field sales reports did not always include enough detail. He expected pages of the zone managers' writing about everything little thing that happened. "How could one know what is going on out in the field without such detailed information?" he asked. I countered that the reports did not match a book or an encyclopedia. And then I asked him a simple question, "Have you taken a look at the divisional rankings? Tell me, please, the name of the division (out of a total of 23) which is in first place?" In my head, I shouted the answer: *The one you are taking over, buster!*

Fast-forward to a week later in the city offices of the company in downtown Munich where this gentleman was being presented as the successor for one of my sales divisions. I am sitting next to my boss when I hear, "People, there will be no exceptions to the rule: All reports, all performance reporting, and all expense reports will be handed in completely filled out—on time. Every field report will not have a single blank missing. I want to see details and more details, even if it takes you weekend time to do so. Otherwise I can't judge your performance, and I can't run this division." I got up, walked out, and went to Paris. Six months later, he had a problem for two reasons: He had substituted exaggerated amounts of written detail in the field reports for personally understanding and mastering those details in the field. Secondly, he had wanted his zone managers to spend more of their time on detailed report writing and less on other issues relevant to successful divisional performance—like going out, knocking on doors, and getting face time with potential customers.

What this man did not understand is that details are not the beginning and end of everything; they are only part, albeit a very important part, of the bigger picture. They are part of what must be a balanced mixture of good leadership, effective and personal motivation, realistic strategies, in-market smarts, simple business models, and passion. You want knowledge and *mastery of the most essential details*, not detail for its own sake.

Even though the smart boss in the previous story used details as the central point and tool of his analysis and in judging project or product viability, he knew that they were not everything. They have their place and you also must, without fail, find where that place is for yourself and your style of operating. Develop your own personal approach to details and what role they play for you: Mastery of detail, being able to discuss all sides of the issues in-depth, being able to move details around, change their sequence or combine them, or quote them 1:1 accurately, in no small way illustrates your understanding of what details mean as a *source and instrument* of power. The facility you possess with detail represents a challenge to those around you to step up and try to match that performance, that knowledge, and that ability. On one hand, you want that challenge out there because you want to know that your organization also recognizes the inherent value of mastering detail. On the other hand, know your detail, walk the walk, and no one will ever get close.

YOU'D LOVE TO, BUT YOU CAN'T KISS 'EM ALL: AVOIDING PRIORITY LOOP-DE-LOOPS

The world is full of opportunity. Even when you as CEO have narrowed down that huge window of opportunity to a more reasonably sized and realistic development plan, you are going to find inside that very framework that you have created more than enough to do. Your mind is loaded with ideas, and every time you get bubbly, *whoops!* There's another project or a program or investment. Is overreach your favorite word? The problem is that the resources, time, personnel, or money, are in no way as abundant as those ideas or concepts you think might move the company forward faster.

The result of "expansive" thinking can be an inordinately large number of projects in the gestation stage, going through the approval process, in the development stage, or just short of the final weeks of work. The company may be humming, but your people are confused and the company is floundering and operating at less than 100 percent efficiency. The problem is that you personally are not spending enough of your time ensuring clear focus in the company, nor are you focused on establishing periodic hard review processes and benchmarks to judge each project's respective viability and value/cost contribution. If you personally mention one specific project one day, your people will pick up on that signal and think "major priority." The next day, you have another major project in mind—another signal, a different priority.

One of the major problems any company faces is the fact that dynamic market forces will alter the originally forecasted preconditions for project or product success. Because some of these projects will take years to complete, you are spinning into an area where you might seriously damage your company, and concurrently run down its resources unnecessarily. You don't want to do something that is going to cost massively in terms of company focus, direction, resource efficiency, and personnel motivation. You don't want to move priorities around spontaneously in response to market shifts, either by announcing that fact officially or by depleting one group's size to give added power to a different project.

Your people pick up on these signals about what you think is hot and what is not as if you were standing next to them with a megaphone. Don't underestimate the effect of this: If the top executive doesn't set immutable priorities, the whole world is still going to move, but not always in the same direction.

Years ago, a senior project engineer and I spoke about what his company was doing in reference to its product development. On a white bulletin board behind his desk, he had written down a list of projects he was working on—12 in all. He commented that he enjoyed the work, but didn't know what was up or what was down on some days. In addition to that, the CEO or his boss would come back and muse about some new idea they had and ask him to work on it. Yes, there was a number 13. That pattern bothered, confused, and frustrated him—as it did his many colleagues who found themselves in the same situation. I commented on the large number of projects, and the fact that there were a lot of eraser smudges on the board, and some not entirely erased letters.

This man was working according to the ever-morphing priorities he was hearing officially, but he was also making the priorities call based on his personal interpretation of what management wanted him to concentrate on. I asked him about project number 11 and how long he would work in a concentrated form on that particular one. His answer: "approximately 30 to 60 minutes, sometimes more—but only when I am not distracted by another project. That can change tomorrow, though."

The three most valuable resources of the company—time, money, and people—were being misused. It is very clear that a CEO has abdicated some of his primary responsibilities if he chooses to run his company this way. With all probability, some combination of the following reasons is behind the problem:

- The CEO has lost sight of the mission for the company (if it ever had one).
- The business model is either not clear or continuously and consciously being subverted or undermined.
- Company results have been less than satisfactory.
- The company is in a "me too" development mode, trying to play product feature catch-up.
- Innovation is not the mantra of the company, because it is almost impossible to have a large number of projects going and have all of them involve only market innovations.
- The product line is too broad.
- The sales force is running the company by bringing in small orders for special technical changes in the existing product, which then turn into mini-projects and lead to mini-production runs.
- The CEO and management are not clear about what the company should be doing so everybody is taking a shot at it.
- The CEO is a fountain of ideas and each of those ideas achieves project status.
- Management has totally missed in its reading of the market and therefore is doing a bad job of allocating company resources. An extreme example of this was a company in which at least one-third of the possible future sales potential for the company existed in one single country, but the subsidiary and its needs for new product were only receiving about 5 to 10 percent of the total product development time resources of the company.

If any of this fits they way your company is operating, you and your company need to do major remedial work. Here are steps to stop your company project lists from gaining weight, your company from losing its way, and your people from facing total confusion:

- As CEO, get *yourself* under control, or someone will put you "under control" for being out of control.
- Establish a set of criteria by which every single project gets approved and resources within the company are allocated to it. These criteria should include a specific and detailed analysis of the contribution of each project to the goals and objectives of the company. The analysis should yield what specific value the project represents in terms of return to the company as well as what contribution it makes to the company's relative position in the market. By setting tight standards in this regard, many of the projects being put on a list for completion will be reduced dramatically, or never even make it onto the list.
- Every current project must be continuously reviewed for its appropriateness and value relative to the company's mission. Available resources and the allocation of resources must be constantly questioned and reviewed. Your management must be in sync with your thinking on the issues of project reevaluation. In judging the continuing relevance of each project, you must take into account potential changes in the company's definition and overriding mission, your current, short-, and middle-term core objectives, the dangers of project inflation, the projected versus actual project results, the current resource allocation and timing constraints needed for overseeing project activity, the role and manning the project management, and changing conditions, both within and outside of the company.
- There must be a *control system* (there are many appropriate software packages available to support this effort) where each and every selected project and its status is measured and "supervised," according to pre-approved benchmarks. You can have some short-cut icons established on your computer so that you can, if you wish, access and acquaint yourself with the real-time progress of the most important ones. If you do not measure and check that progress, your people will not consider those projects to be of major importance. They will

think there are others that exist somewhere in the system that are more important.

- Each of your department heads and subsidiary managers should know that you expect absolute discipline in keeping all project records current. When you click a project icon, the last date of entry you want to see is the day before. No exceptions.

- You can have hundreds of projects in a big company and do just fine, but the company as a whole can and should have only four or five top-tier projects, the nature of which will, in all likelihood, involve many of the talent resources in your company. Be sure that you use your mission and business model as the main source of those criteria you will use to measure which project alternatives find their way onto the company's main priority list. No question that your top management should be involved in the analysis and choice of these projects and help in ensuring that all managers in the company are fully aware of the importance of these priority projects and their meaning for the future of the company.

- Focus your company and its talents on those areas where the most value creation for the company will take place. Be sure you have agreed with your people how value is to be defined. This is a good test and loop-back-to-the-beginning check for you to determine if the prior discussions with your management on the definition of the company, its mission, its business model, and its short- and middle-term objectives bore fruit, or were useless.

Following the steps outlined here, you should be in a position to eliminate most, if not all, of the confusion, lack of direction, waste of resources, and questions about the current condition of your personal clearness of thought, purpose, and direction. The one alternative has you running in place or falling back, the other moving the company sharply and aggressively forward.

THE LAWYERS SAY YOU CAN'T LOSE. YOUR SIXTH SENSE IS FORECASTING VIOLENT THUNDERSTORMS.

No need to tell you how important lawyers are to the integrity and safety and protection of your company and its stakeholders. No need to tell you how often you must consult with them on myriad matters—from the wording of a single letter, to a complicated contract, from advertising text content, to product warranty guarantees.

Because you have been at this for a while, you know you actually don't do anything in the public domain without passing it to your lawyers, be they internal, external, or both, for their approval or doubts. Without their expensive, time-consuming work, you, your company, and your stakeholders could be on dangerous ground.

So now something has come up that has you *really* worried. Let's say your company has been sued by another company in a breach-of-contract matter. Several months ago, you signed a preliminary contract to take over a much smaller but successful company in your industry. What a deal! From a strategic point of view, you have wanted to do this for a long time: You have coveted this company, its distribution network, its product lines (which dovetail well with your lines from a price point and product feature point of view), as well as its new product pipeline. You know some of their management and generally think highly of them.

Contained in the contract you signed, there is the usual escape clause, but the contract also calls for your company to pay the other company a large separation fee if you decide not to go through with the deal. Financing has been arranged and due diligence is being completed. Stockholder approval should be clear after the next special stockholders meeting.

Several months have passed. You are waiting for the final due diligence report which should be in your office today. But the chief negotiator from your company and your auditors have asked you for a private meeting. They come in with their black books, computers, and very serious faces: There is a big problem. The auditors have discovered what they consider to be some major discrepancies in the value of the other company's inventories. Their accounts receivables at the divisional level in several countries where the company operates look like they are being eaten by hungry moths. Several of the most important of the benchmark numbers to be met contractually by the company you are acquiring are not even close to what they should be. Your lead manager tells you that he thinks those numbers will never have any basis in fact.

On top of all of this, your auditors have discovered some unusual big cash transfers to places you have never heard of, and off-shore locations are being mentioned as having been in play. There are signs that government regulatory constraints may have been ignored or just half-heartedly adhered to. Fraud and misrepresentation could be in the air.

In your view, your company conducted the negotiations in good faith; apparently, however, the value and the practices of the company you are acquiring have been misrepresented. And the other company's current policies and practices, and the reality of these practices in their daily operations, contain major downside risks for your company, should you acquire it. That's the content of the first five minutes of the discussion. The next five minutes contain a fast run-through of your company's obligations it if backs out. Big money must be paid to the other side unless your company can prove that it has been defrauded. This is getting worse by the minute. Call the lawyers.

This is their hour and they are up to it. Back out. Stop worrying about the money you will have to pay them; stop worrying about them countersuing. They have no basis for it. The auditors buzz and nod their heads. So do you. You pay the other company CEO the courtesy of a phone call telling him the facts, followed up by a letter approved by your lawyers that outlines the reasons for your action. You are no longer going through with the deal, and are not going to pay the separation fee.

The U.S. mail still works well these days, and a short time later, you have a countersuit on your desk for breach-of-contract. You read it and swallow hard because in its contents, you discover that that perfect picture you had of the quality of *your* auditors' work and of many of the other due diligence research issues are not turning out to be so perfect. Mistakes have been made. Some of them can be rationalized, but others appear to be serious with negative consequences for your company. In fact, if one is to believe the suit, a number of those things that caused you to back away from the contract were discussed, and plans made to resolve them during very "detailed negotiations and discussions with (lots of names of your people are listed with their titles)." Even worse, some of the legal points of the case, which you had wanted to discuss more thoroughly (but your lawyers felt were not central), have become major attack points from the other side. Visions of massive damages dance in your head. No phone call from the company CEO you had spoken to out of courtesy several weeks ago. The line has gone dead.

The lawyers stay the course. They check the contents of the suit, do some back-channel checking, interviewing, some considering, some thinking, some consulting with you several times, and announce that your backing out strategy and decision is still valid. There are some risks involved, but they are well within the realm of acceptable. Their recommendation remains the same: Get out and defend.

Fortunately, your sixth sense is working overtime; you have one of those vague, uneasy feelings. You remember another instance where you were involved in some serious litigation involving a problematic takeover. Your lawyers had supposedly informed you about everything relating to the legal aspects of the case. You were informed that you had been completely and thoroughly informed about the law and every aspect of the case. You, of course, had provided every relevant bit of information you were asked for and what you felt could have some consequence for the case at hand. But after the case had begun, you noticed certain sticky issues in the written communications between your company and the opposite side. They were points your lawyers had partially missed or weighed too lightly, different legal points involving precedence cases—tactical points that were strong and convincing.

What you learned from that was never depend completely on what your lawyers are telling you, nor allow them to set the strategy for the case in isolation. *You have to think along with them.* You have to get involved in the detail. You have to question the underlying assumptions they are using to arrive at their conclusions. They don't see everything; they can't. They depend on you for relevance, completeness of information, as well as hard questions. They know law; you know the company and most likely have a very different perspective on the whole legal situation.

In the case at hand, you are already exposed and will have to fight without a key benefit that could have helped you to make a better decision than just canceling the contract. That benefit is in knowing what the other side is possibly going to do to you. If you find yourself in this position and want to support your sixth sense, then do the following: reverse field. Find a lawyer who will analyze the case as though he's your opponent. Make it his job to tell you why your company has no chance of winning your suit against the other side. This may not be the case at all, but you want and need to see the worst case possible and under what conditions or circumstances that worst case situation could become reality.

This action won't please your current law firm. They will argue that all points, positive and negative, have been more than adequately considered in their analysis and communications on the subject at hand. But there is very big money involved here, and a mistake or a misinterpretation could be disastrous for your company and stakeholders. Have the "opposing" lawyer dig hard and even deeper than your other lawyers already have. His focus should be on taking your company down and, in addition, embarrassing you. You will read his brief and immediately thereafter start sweating.

What else will he do? He will give you some very serious and worrisome insight into what the other company is in all probability hearing from *their* legal advisors. That has infinite value for you and your decision-making process. In consulting with and listening carefully to this particular lawyer, you will most likely be in a state of constant concern because the points he is putting on the table appear to be highly relevant for the *opposite side's* chance of winning. In other words, these points and facts were not substantial parts of the initial analysis of the case, nor were they the major reasons for your law firm's subsequent written recommendation to use the escape clause and not to pay the fee.

It is better to go outside of your current law firm arrangement to find such a person. Go to a law firm where no conflicts-of-interest exist and where the firm has no problem in taking a look at a "colleague's" work.

It costs more. It takes more time. It creates some big ego problems, and perhaps conflict, particularly with your current law firm and the lawyers with whom you work. But think about losing the case and what that would mean.

This "extra" step goes a long way toward protecting the interests of your company and your stakeholders with all the legal and logical means and procedures available to you. Choosing to proceed in this fashion arms you to fight the battle in court or perhaps in any negotiations during any judicial proceedings aimed at resolving the conflict. The other position is to seek a negotiated settlement and thereby admit some culpability in the whole affair, which is not pretty. Whatever you decide, your job is to make that call. Use all the forces and sources you have at your disposal. Then and only then have you done everything to achieve the lowest possible risk quotient for your legal battle.

NEGOTIATING CONTRACTS: POKER FACE NOT REQUIRED

Let's get rid of a little bit of silliness right at the beginning. You just sat down at the table where some serious negotiating is about to begin. In play is an acquisition or the purchase of a license or a factory property, for example. You say you are there for "informational" purposes or "to see if there is the possibility of a deal" or "to analyze the possible alternative courses of actions available to us."

If you are sitting at the table and preparations for this meeting started weeks ago, on both sides, then the only person you are kidding with this talk is yourself. You make your side of the negotiating table appear just a little ridiculous and disingenuous. You are there because your company is interested in a deal, and because it is you that is there, *seriously* interested.

Assuming you *are* serious, there are a number of things you should keep foremost in your mind when you enter into the negotiation phase.

People and facts influence both deal content and chances of successful negotiations.

Know as precisely as possible what motives or possible pressures are driving the sellers. Ascertain how strong these relative motives are, which ones they consider the most valuable, and which ones they might be willing to concede once the hard bargaining starts. Do they have a financial or emotional threshold of pain, and if so, where is it? Play the preparatory game as if you were on the opposite side of the negotiating table.

This analysis is easier said than done, but it is the precondition for your having a shot at success in negotiations. There are, of course, many ways to determine what the other side is thinking and why they themselves or their investment bankers are at the negotiating table. Fundamentally, it's the same reason you are: They want a deal. But their weighting of deal makers and deal breakers, their personality, break-off points, personal agendas, and timing constraints may be entirely different from yours. Not the best preconditions for successful negotiations and the closing of a deal if you don't know what those differences are and can't plan your tactics around them.

You have a number of avenues open to you to get this kind of information. On the personal side, you may know the people on the other side already, and, if you don't, you will certainly be able to find people who do and discuss with them (if the confidentiality of the negotiations doesn't stop you from doing this) what kind of people they are. The tone of the e-mails and other communication with you will also give you some indication of what kind of people you are dealing with, as well as the contents of the list of questions they may have sent you on certain issues. Their public statements, possibly on this subject, but certainly on entirely other issues will also help to round out the picture you need. Gathering facts about the company, its strengths and weaknesses, possible reasons and motivation for doing a deal, and its past history in negotiating other similar deals are all activities that should present you with few, if any, difficulties.

Know exactly what you want to buy, why, how much you'll buy, and how you are going to pay for it.

Have a firm grasp of these points in advance of the negotiations. You may think this is standard stuff, but that's not exactly true. Your lawyers will have already had a chance to read and advise you on the content of the letter of intent that you may have signed previous to the start of negotiations, but they are the lawyers, and you are the operations guy. So make sure that you have your part completely memorized and backed up by solid data and analysis. You may know why you want to buy what is being offered, but part of your job is to ensure that everything that you intend to purchase is listed in fine detail in any contract you sign, as well as backed up by documentation of clear ownership. Make sure you know exactly what you are *not* getting with the purchase. Too many deals have been fouled up after the fact, even with the best of contracts prepared by professional help, by there not being complete clarity on what is in fact being transferred with what rights to the new owner.

Be sure that you have established a corridor with a maximum price you will be willing to pay. Know *why* that is the maximum price. In addition, for each price gradient on the way up the negotiating ladder, you should have an additional predetermined benefit or set of benefits you would require in the package in order for you to even consider accepting any higher price gradient.

Make sure there is an operational and value-added fit between what you have now as a company and what you may be adding to it. This means modeling and calculating in detail all relevant operational and strategic synergies, as well as the effect any deal will have on the employees in your company.

Make sure that you have a number of creative financing alternatives thought out in advance, and that their financing is *definitively* secure before you start your negotiations or put any deal offer on the table. Knowing you have the money and can in fact do the deal is a tremendous advantage and psychologically important when the final and last negotiations have started. It means you are ready to deal and you have the ammunition to do it.

Be prepared to get up from the table and walk away.

Regardless of the good faith in the efforts, a breakdown might occur. The negotiating becomes cumbersome; there is a loss of momentum. Doubt has crept into the negotiating room. Perhaps some demands have been made that were not part of the original package. You may have caused this problem yourself by reaching, or overreaching, for a much better deal. But if you are the buyer, and the possibility of your achieving some major benefits from any possible deal is rapidly shrinking because of demands from the selling side, be prepared to walk out of the room and away from the deal. This is not something you decide to do in a moment of pique, anger, or annoyance. Rather, you should make very clear, at the very start of the negotiating process, where you and your company stand on the major points on the table. Should you, at some point, perceive that these limits were being ignored or pushed back, then this fact would require you to step back from any further negotiations. This is a marker you must put in the sand.

Of course, this could be a negotiating tactic on your part or something worse: a serious rupture in the negotiating process. Whatever it is, it very clearly puts on the table what must take place for a deal to be done. After that, it is up to both parties, and to you in particular who has taken the walk, to find a way back up the path to restarting the negotiations.

Focus intensely on conducting comprehensive due diligence or you may have just made the worst deal of your life.

How many times have you heard of major due diligence exercises taking place, deals being closed, and then a whole collection of negative things being discovered after the fact? Whatever can be said about accountants and financial analysts, they are not operations people; they will potentially miss any number of things you would most likely see if you personally were to go through the books or visit all of what you are purchasing. Whatever the deal, big or small, you must be personally involved in this process. No matter what the time constraints of the deal, do *not* allow yourself to be pushed into a quick-look-and-approve situation. If you miss something, or your people miss something, your potentially great deal could become the worst deal of your life. And if you find something that turns the deal into a burden, then back off. Use the precisely worded clauses you have included in the preliminary contract you signed that allows you to walk away.

Manage public and employee relations when the cat is out of the bag.

When the deal is done, and a public announcement has been agreed upon, the mechanics involved in making the deal public shouldn't be too difficult. Your greater concern is the internal public relations effort. If the deal is a win-win for both employees and company, then there will be time enough for celebration and planning the further steps necessary to make the deal work its magic.

If, however, the deal is a winner, but will necessitate personnel displacements, terminations, or organizational shifts within your own company, articulate them as clearly and as compassionately as you can in advance. It will be worse for your people if they don't know what is in play than if they know it upfront so they can deal with it.

Woe to the CEO who rushes a deal and then turns around and tries to stop the avalanche of rumors and worry accompanying his official announcement relating to negotiations or the conclusion of a deal. That smile you are wearing isn't going to last very long when you watch your company descend into turmoil because you ignored a basic principle involved in such exercises: Make sure your people are solidly behind what you are doing before the public announcement. Achieving a consensus that you have negotiated an advantageous deal for the company, in spite of the possible pain for parts of the company, starts well in advance of the official announcement. Many of your people know what is going on and they are already hard at work figuring out the consequences for everything and everybody. They may be more realistic than you think about the need for changes.

So if there is no confidentiality clause hindering it, or no required partial information blackout, then be open to your people and tell them what is going on. And if there are alternatives, say that they exist, but emphasize that the overall mantra and policy of the company will be to guard and safeguard the interests of the stakeholders. And because the stakeholders know they only have a company if they have a competent and motivated team in place, your people will know that they and their interests are *also* being taken into consideration, along with all of the other important factors involved.

If you can almost taste the deal, you will overpay.

I knew the CEO of a consumer goods company in England who was negotiating to buy back the distribution rights the company had contractually given away years before to another company outside of the country. This was a "must-do" deal with many benefits for the company and a resulting clean control of its destiny in the distribution of its products around the world. On paper, company prospects for a deal looked good after a few hasty calculations, a positive pay-back analysis (buy back price against future net additional earnings), and an offer that was three times what another company was offering for the very same rights.

Unfortunately, the numbers were not good enough. Late in the afternoon, the deal was done, and there was celebration into the night. But it wasn't the English company that was exuberant. Sure, the distribution rights came back to the parent company, but the real winner was the company selling them back. Management had sent every signal they could that they wanted a deal. They just waited until the conclusion of the negotiations to add "at any price."

You don't have a printing press available in the basement to print that kind of money. The world will not come to an end if the deal doesn't go through. You might be annoyed and frustrated, but think about a time down the road when you are trying to add up the benefits and compare them to the costs of your overpaid purchase deal. No matter how you may finesse the numbers, you most likely aren't going to like what you see when all the calculations are done.

Key Priorities

- You may think that no effective leadership is possible in a situation where there appears to be daily problems, no consensus achievable, exigencies, emergencies, blockages, agendas, or breakdowns. Either these issues run the show or you do. Effective leadership requires that you cut through all of them and lead, even if at times some of your people won't like the direct way you use to do it.

- You are a CEO at an interesting period of time. Unfortunately, because there are so many opportunities out there, your company might find itself drowning in interesting projects with no resources left on which to draw. Focus is a short word, but one with a lot of power. Establish priorities for your growth and don't deviate from the project choices you have made.

- If you want to continue to use those strengths that got you to where you are today, concentrate your approach on two points: You know the questions to ask and you know how to judge the quality of the answers. You don't need anything more than that.

- Micro management is not entirely out. Forgotten or ignored details can be killers. Used correctly, knowledge of detail can provide you with an enormous amount of power not only to lead more effectively, but also to ensure effective execution of your company strategy. Link yourself up with the key operational or lynch pin project details that will make the difference in your company.

- Working with your legal team (either in-house or from outside) can be fruitful and intellectually challenging, but also dangerous. Lawyers take positions, but they also have their doubts. However, if something goes wrong, they aren't responsible; you are. If your sixth sense is working overtime, then those doubts about the validity of your case or your chances of winning the case have to be eliminated. Find yourself a pit bull with a contrary, second opinion *outside* of the circle of your current legal advisors.

- The ties that bind can contain a lot of good for the future of your company. Getting to the point where your signature confirms those ties can be a convoluted, and sometimes interesting, game of poker: two cards up, one card down. Respect the rules of engagement, don't hurry your due diligence, and be ready to walk if the benchmarks you have established for a deal are not in sight.

Chapter 4

Earning Your Effective Leader Merit Badge

With your appointment to the position of CEO, you might be assuming that it's a done deal. You have been dreaming of and preparing for this day for years. Sure, you have to lead the company. Sure, there are many problems waiting for you to solve. Sure, you're going to have more gray hair on the day you retire than on the day you started your new job. But be careful. Although you may not officially have to worry about your appointment anymore, that doesn't eliminate the need to be consistently effective and convincing—*from the first day onwards.*

Starting the New Job: Minutes That Count and Reverberate

That first day in your new position is full of promise and the most opportunity to positively impact your future work in the company. You feel the pride, love the welcoming handshakes, and enjoy the really great meetings. Why should two months down the road be any different? But it is exactly that period of the first two or three months that contain the most danger and the most opportunity for you and your work in your company. Your challenge is how to organize your time in those months, prepare in advance for them, go about making the kind of impression you want to make, set priority points, and judge the culture and inner workings of the organization so you can use those factors to your benefit in setting the right tone. How you manage these first few months will have long-lasting consequences for you, your image, and your power.

You are a known entity. Your resume and the successes contained therein are known. People have read the publicity and the public relations releases. Someone down the hall knows you from earlier, and has passed on his impression and knowledge of you. In short, you have already been introduced before you have had a chance to shake one hand.

There are things other than such introductions, however, that need your attention before the first day on the new job. Part of what you should do to prepare is to interview several of your colleagues who have faced similar "introductory" situations. Ask them to give you their take on their first several months, how they prepared themselves mentally for it, and went about ordering the necessary steps and activities that were required for both CEO and company personnel to move forward quickly and effectively.

Your colleagues will tell you both what worked well for them in those first few months and what didn't. What you will very likely hear is a recommendation to pick a major area of concentration, one "signal move," that will help you to put down a successful marker from the beginning of your tenure. Assuming proper preparation and execution, what this marker will do is underline your abilities, as well as put some proof on the table that you know what you are doing. Definitely put this suggestion on the list. It is a good first step toward building credibility for yourself as the new CEO.

Beware the tendency to make this period more complicated than it really is, though. If you think KISS (keep it simple, stupid), you will realize there are only two overriding issues with which you should be immediately concerned: information flow and orientation, and surviving the first five minutes of your first meeting with your top management team.

While you will have spent time in advance of your first day reviewing a large amount of information relative to the company and its position in the market, now that you are officially on board, you will listen face-to-face to what your staff views as important for the company going forward. You will be interested in knowing their immediate and mid-term needs and concerns and want to be apprised of any urgent issues that could affect the company. These could include, for example, a number of operational or strategic issues, upcoming merger negotiations, potential large-customer sales issues, production delays affecting sales promotions planned within the next week, the cash position and cash flow in the company, payables and receivables positions, or legal situations needing your immediate attention. You will also let everyone know exactly what subjects and discussion points you are looking for in any reports or presentations you ask them to prepare. You don't want a hodgepodge of different reports, some short because the executive writing that report is a no-nonsense kind of guy, or too long because the executive's writing style is blatantly stream of consciousness.

The surviving issue, however, is the one that *really* counts. You are certainly aware that it is the employees of the company and their support that are going to be the decisive factors in how well you can integrate yourself into the company and fulfill your mission. You are thinking two or three months is enough time to get these important factors in place. You are *way* off the mark. You might be done after the *first five or 10 minutes of your first set of meetings in the first week.*

What this means is simple: during the first few meetings, your people will have a good chance to look at and size you up. They will watch you come into the room for the first time, and note the words you chose in addressing them. You will be able to almost hear the unspoken opinions of these people locking in like watertight doors on a submarine. For all practical purposes, the first two or three months you had intended to use in order to cement your position and bond with your people weren't ever really available to you. The first and immediate impression you make on your people and their read on you will shape the relationship you have with each and every one of them for a long time.

What questions are your management people going to have in their minds as they sit there and experience you for the first time?

- Who is this person I am looking at and listening to?
- What is he *really* saying to us? How is he saying it?

- What is his philosophy? What does he believe in? What is important to him?
- Is he intransigent in his opinions?
- What is he going to be expecting from me and from my team? What can I expect from him?
- Based on what I am seeing and hearing, can I successfully work with this person?
- Is this someone with whom I have shared beliefs or views, which could constructively influence the quality of our working relationship?
- Are we going to be able to find common ground in arriving at important tactical and strategic decisions affecting the company?

Nothing but answers to these questions will interest your management team. What they do not want to hear, nor should they hear, is anything about your past successes; about what your mama said when you called her with the good news; hard-nosed warnings about what will happen if "we don't shape this place up;" a list of all the things that you are going to change; about the economy going south on us just when we are turning over a new leaf; or how you never dreamed you would ever find yourself in such a position. Turn that off—all of it.

Every one of the questions the attendees are asking themselves revolves around personal relationships, impressions, philosophy, and feelings about you as a human being and as a leader. The players in this theater event are you and them. Every single one of these people will leave their first meeting with you, turn to their neighbor or colleague in the hall, and ask the one big question: "What do you think?"

During the first few months of your tenure, you will come into contact with many more hundreds or perhaps thousands of people in the company. One by one, they will listen to and observe you, but with one difference. These people will already have heard *everything* about you. They will "know" you and have an opinion about you. If it's positive, you are on your way. If you blew it in those first few minutes of the first week, you have a serious, long-term problem. Or maybe it will only be a short-term one if the board decides the problem is *too* serious.

Therefore, when you start to prepare for those critical first two months, consider how to electrify your employees' imagination and their feeling for the future of the company. Certainly, they will be waiting for your thoughts on these subjects. But what you, first of all, must provide them with are immediate and credible answers to their unvoiced questions concerning you as a leader and as a person. The Germans have a well-turned phrase for this situation: *nur der erste Eindruck zaehlt, der zweite ist nur die Bestaetigung—oder die Nichtbestaetigung—des ersten Eindruckes.* It means only first impressions count; the second impression has only the function of confirming or not confirming the first impression.

You Finally Made It. Now How Do You Hold Onto It?

Call your mother. Spread the good news. E-mail that professor who once said you'd chosen the wrong profession or made the wrong initial job selection. Get yourself dressed up for your public relations and announcement photo.

You look around and you see lots of to-dos. The job is enormous. However, there is one special thing out there that you should pay attention to, not only at the start of your work, but also during the whole span of your tenure as CEO. Its name is humility. The German language is particularly colorful in describing this situation: *du solltest bloss nicht abheben* or in loosely translated English, *don't let all of this go to your head.* You recognize the fact that that your hat size was 7 3/8 before all of this. You need to make sure it is the same size when you walk in on your first day in the new job. And that it stays that same size for the duration of your time with the company.

It can be tempting to blow off a little steam, to do the strut every once in a while. But nobody wants to watch your ego in constant action, or hear a 30-minute speech with one minute of content. Nobody wants to hear you frame every success the company has achieved as your success. Nobody wants to see you earning ever-bigger amounts of money while reducing salaries or personnel count.

And certainly, no one wants to hear about your trips on the private company jet or walk into your office and think he has walked into your personal shrine. There's nothing wrong with a few pictures on your desk or wall, and maybe even a letter or two, but learn the value of moderation, or you are off-message.

One only has to think of recent examples of the auto executives, who completely missed the fact that it was totally out of place to travel by company jet to Washington for hearings on possible taxpayer support for their companies. Their mindset didn't cause them to reflect on what possible damage their "standard" way of thinking would do to themselves, their image, their credibility, and the companies they represented.

But how do you remain continuously and firmly planted on corporate Mother Earth, and yet still be able to do a little of the dance? One thing is clear: You are not going to start solving this problem by repeatedly launching your own power trips. You will not be respected. Power and respect go to those who show they are not always infallible, who show that they, in fact, do have certain weaknesses or frailties, and that they also are not afraid to let others see. Power goes to those who show they understand and respect the feelings and worries of their employees. Showing you are human and that you understand humility beats those ego trips hands down, every time.

I knew the CEO of the third-largest department store chain in Germany, who relished giving a speech to the assembled guests every time there was a major department store opening. Because my company was selling product to his company, I was invited often to hear him talk at these early evening "store opening" parties. One of them took place in Munich.

Before leading a tour through the store, the CEO spoke almost in monotone about the hard work and planning that had gone into making the Munich store what it had become. He thanked people from the mayor of the city and members of the planning commission down to the workers. It was a boilerplate speech. His audience talked while he talked. At least the champagne and canapés were good.

All of a sudden, he switched to other subjects. He started talking about the human side of store openings. He spoke of the people who had contributed to making the store a success, and those who had shown him a better way to do certain things. He related some of his personal experiences in the retail business, and spoke gratefully about the training and support he had received from several mentors. He cited those who had helped him when he was inexperienced and had stood in awe of large department stores and their opening ceremonies. He spoke of some of the mistakes he had made along the way, which he avoided when creating the store he was opening that evening. And he told the crowd of some of the disappointments he had experienced along the path of his career.

In the center atrium where the festivities took place, where there had been background chatter competing against his boilerplate niceties, you could now have heard a pin drop. There was absolute quiet, except for the sole voice of a man, who was revealing that he was more than just the unreachable and un-fazed CEO of a large company. He showed that he was a human being, with frailties and emotions, with disappointments and aspirations.

In turn, the guests reacted to this man in a very human way. They thought to themselves, "I am like that person. I have made mistakes like that. I can iden-tify with what he is talking about, even if my life experiences aren't exactly the same as his." That struck a nerve with the listeners—and they listened.

There will be many instances where you will be conducting meetings, ex-pressing your opinion, giving speeches, thanking your employees, and making presentations. These are the times where you must be formal, but there will also be times when you will have an opportunity to show humility and your human side. It does *not* mean that you tell self-deprecating stories to show that you, too, have the same weaknesses and suffer defeats as everyone else does. Just like a polished surface, a personal image that is so smooth that it is simply not capable of giving anyone in your environment the chance to "latch onto you" is definitely counterproductive for your image and your leadership. People need to know that you feel, suffer, and doubt. They don't want to know this because they want to have something they can lord over you (with the exception of those who want to undermine you). They want to know this be-cause they identify with humanness; they bond with it.

Keeping a good distance between yourself and your people by showing only the polished façade you have created is the easy way out. Do you think this is CEO-like? Perfect from every angle? What are you hiding? Being human is the most natural thing in the world. It doesn't cost anything and it is a winner every time.

AVOIDING IVORY TOWER MYOPIA: KEEP YOUR HIKING BOOTS CLOSE AT HAND

Remember the days when you were a manager in the field, interacting with your customers, running an offshoot operation in a foreign country, or developing your successful business plans? Those were the days! The universe wasn't too large and occasionally there was time for a late-afternoon chat with your team. Now you are at the top. But has anything really changed? Yes and no. There are certain things you will want to continue: reliable, respected, and forward-thinking; control of your numbers; showing integrity and good work ethic; talking your vision in fewer than 150 words; and telling a couple of good stories to make your point. Going forward, however, one of the things you are definitely going to need in order to lead successfully is *right back down the road you used on the way up*. Let's examine why.

Coming up the trail, you knew your market and the market weaknesses of your company intimately. You had a strategy, a team, and direction, and you knew your customers. You also knew the strengths and weaknesses of your business and could rattle off the names and respective performance of your top 25 accounts. Now, all of a sudden, you are out of direct contact with all of that.

Now you participate in high-level briefings and conferences. Not only are you in that "lonely" limbo of the CEO position, but you are also substantially cut off from having some of the most important information you need: a solid and substantive feeling for the basics of your business, the day-to-day push and pull of the market, possible problems slowing down company progress, and contact with the people who use your products on a continuing basis.

This is a slippery situation. You may have confidence in the managers who run those functions and trust in checks and balances and reviews, but your knowledge has only a two-dimensional character. You need to stop and ask yourself why you have been successful in your life and made it to where you are. Once upon a time, you were one with that road and knew it intimately; this knowledge served you well, and as CEO, you are starting to realize that it is still must. Without that intimate feeling for your business, you are going to be operating in a danger zone. You will not be able to fully engage your divisional or your regional managers, or your vice or senior vice presidents in substantive discussions about the business. You will become dependent upon second-hand information—possibly filtered, incomplete, falsely weighted, politicized, and therefore, misleading. Your field, market, and customer knowledge will be from the past, *not* the present, or the near future.

The situation becomes even more complicated when you are a newcomer CEO. You may be listening, you may be reading and questioning. But you are missing the company-specific feel of the road up. Without that, you could possibly still be doing all the "right" things, yet missing or misinterpreting a potentially large number of serious and important signals coming to you. If you want to manage meaningfully and effectively—if you want to be a *three-dimensional* CEO—then there is no Plan B for what the smart CEO must do: Even though there are some who will say "this is not CEO-like," a part of you must remain that middle manager, that person on the road on the way up. There simply must be a certain amount of your time allocated to immersing yourself in the guts of your business, for visiting and talking to your managers in the field, your customers, and truck drivers and packers on the shipping lines. Keep these ideas in mind when you decide to revisit that road.

Don't just do the usual by-the-numbers visit, including discussions behind closed doors, or a mammoth PowerPoint presentation. Don't just show up and give a speech, and then disappear to the next appointment. Do more than just take a plant tour and whisper sweet nothings about the performance of a particular machine. Meet with your production line or divisional people and ask them what they need and what they would do if they themselves were running the place for a week.

Ask people how you—personally—and the company are performing. Ask them about their understanding of the current and long-term company strategy. Ask them what they would do if they were CEO for a day. Want some more interesting reactions? Bounce off of them some of those great new sales or service ideas your headquarters staff is currently talking about. You might be quite startled by what you will hear.

CEOs are responsible for strategy, for clear and transparent goals, for organizational strength and balance. How successful can you be in formulating and implementing proper strategies if the information you are using to establish those strategies has already been filtered or even politicized before it reaches you? Respect for the CEO, and for her credibility, stems not only from intelligence or organized thinking or precise Business 101 analysis. It stems from good results, borne by accurate information. Your people will give you that kind of respect, if they believe that the guidance and strategic direction you give are fundamentally sound and relevant. You will deliver that during your next trip to one of your operating divisions.

Key Priorities

- You have a great feeling starting the new job as CEO, but be careful. The first five minutes you spend with your management may be the first step toward *losing* that feeling. How you act and what you say will impact the answer to the question everyone will be asking after your first appearance: What do you think?

- As CEO, you know the mechanics of the job and you are good at establishing strategy. What you really need to be good at are the "warm and fuzzies." The first step here is showing your people that you are human and have the same cares and concerns and anxieties they do. Showing your human side is the leadership glue that bonds people to you and promotes success.

- You did a great job on the way to your current position. You were right in the middle of things. That is also where you still need to be when you are CEO if you want to continue being able to make proper and effective judgments about the plans and programs designed to carry your company forward.

Chapter 5

SPEED BUMPS

You operate in an environment that is neither uniform in character, nor without danger. It's not summer every day. There are seasons and that means there are days when you might not be too enthusiastic about putting a foot outside of your front door. Nevertheless, as CEO, you have to be a man or woman for all seasons, and counter, work with, and overcome everything those seasons could possibly throw at you. So roll up your sleeves and take a look at some of the difficult issues or situations that require you not only to leave the house every day, but also demand that you confront them in a direct, and sometimes hard, fashion.

POWER POLITICS AND PALACE REVOLUTIONS: THE HUNS INSIDE THE GATES

Up to now, you may have had free reign in running companies. Relatively few problems with your top management plagued you, and politics inside of the company were at a minimum. Now you face an entirely different situation, and it will test you sharply. Your only challenge is not your company's competition. The reality is that, the minute you open the door to your office on your first day as CEO, you potentially have people inside the company who viscerally dislike, or even hate you, and want you out of the company as quickly as possible. While this sort of situation is more the exception than the rule, it is not going too far to assume that, at some point in your career, you will unfortunately encounter this kind of push back to your arrival as new CEO.

Not only do these people hate you (or at least reject you), but they will also have already begun to enlist others within the company whom they want on their side against you. The machinery is running hot before you even sit down at your desk.

The reasons behind this kind of a response to your presence can be numerous:

- Someone else had aspirations for the job, didn't get it, and concluded, after "serious reflection," that the selection process had serious flaws. Their hopes had been dashed, and it wasn't their fault. Blame must fall on someone, and, because you're the greatest beneficiary of the flawed system, you automatically become the biggest target.
- Your supposed style of leadership or rumored plans could be the problem: No one really knows what you are going to do, how you are going to act, or what policies you are going to follow, but everybody "knows" it in spite of that—and they also know it will be "bad," and therefore has to be stopped.
- Somebody in the company knows you from another company situation, or from within the company, and got to know you during your climb up the ladder; his memories of you are more like nightmares. He may even have worked for you previously and, right or wrong, he has decided that once is enough (you might think the same thing).
- There is concern you are going to bring in a new team and replace some of the current management. This could involve some people from your previous company or totally new hires from outside.
- Your real or rumored lifestyle—or its purported nature or the publicity surrounding it—may offend certain people in the company.

- You seem so different from the beloved previous leader that you can't be any good. Another possible strike against you: You come from another industry and don't understand what "our industry and our culture" are all about.

Most likely, you could add more to this list without much thought.

As usual, the first step in solving a problem is in knowing that you have one. And as a new CEO, it is possible to have this problem, no matter how competent, respectful, likeable, intelligent, and accomplished you may be. You may think you are coming into the position to do the usual things like battle the competition, perhaps reorganize things, and expand the market for your products and services. Trusting in your nice persona, you may think that your personality contribution to achieving victories in those areas will win over the recalcitrant members of your new staff. The reality is a totally different one: You are already at war with some of your people. And they don't care what you do.

These people need to know that war is at hand.

Step One: Identify and study them.

What are they thinking and doing? Who are they influencing? What, specifically, are they trying to do to undermine you? How do you interpret or judge the low grade buzz on their "chances" to cause some real harm?

Step Two: Neutralize them.

You may think that they may fall in line if you work your magic on them, but that is a false assumption. Once you have identified them, and tried that magic, you will almost always discover that you have done nothing more than put a Band-Aid on a non-healing wound. This is especially true if the cause of the animosity is their envy that you got the job instead of them or their top pick. Your actions may mask or temporarily relieve the problem, but remain aware of the fact that, should you at any time stumble or hit a weak period in your performance, these people will most likely be back in force, Band-Aid or not. They could hit you in your weakened state and push you further down, perhaps by running to a board member with whatever "dirt" they can gather against you. They are dangerous.

No need to feel sorry about having to be really tough if you experience this kind of thing; get used to it. You may like things in gray because they are comfortable and easy to deal with, but here—and in any similar survival situation—you are dealing with black and white. You can accept no middle ground. Decisiveness is required in such a situation.

If this guidance reminds you of the old phrases "If you are not my friend, you are my enemy" and "if you are not my enemy, you are my friend," then you are not far away from the truth of the matter. Unfortunately, you are most likely going to be spending a part of your valuable time on these issues instead of addressing operational problems and the growth of the company. Don't get things confused here: You don't want "yes men" of any gender in the company, slavishly doing your will. Exactly the opposite. You want dialogue, substantive criticism, and new ideas.

You don't want the insidious disruption wrought by malcontents and their personal attacks. Problems such as these could very likely be ongoing, not just things to be taken care of at the beginning of your tenure. So don't bother harboring any doubts about wasting your time. It is part of the job. If there are some Huns inside your company, you need to take care of the problem and move on.

Think about it in the context of operational concerns. Part of your ability to do your job is in the process of being undermined by people who don't like you or reject your leadership. By taking the time now to meet the problem head on, you contribute directly to the growth of the company by boosting your chances of achieving success in what you plan to do. You owe it to the stakeholders and the people in your company—and to yourself.

The two-step process of identifying and neutralizing the negative factors is proactive, not passive. During your whole tenure as CEO, you need to be alert to how people respond to you and, at the same time, have enough time to size them up. As part of the neutralizing step, you have to take action that is direct, and often final. Because everyone knows the best defense is frequently the offense, you need to exploit the value of a preemptive strike. After identification, you need action, not hesitation.

Use both facts and intuition in your efforts to identify who these people are. What do they tell you about who you can trust, who can be swayed, and who has already laid down a bet that you will be forced to drink the hemlock?

Obvious Choices in the Identification Process

It is probable you will be aware immediately of some of the problem people in your new organization, particularly if they were the ones who wanted or were considered for your job in the first place. How were the handshakes when you walked into the first meeting you held on your first day? What did the eyes say to you? Did someone not meet your gaze? There are whole books written about body language, and there is one area in which they could help you.

It is also probable that some of them will not wait to attack you openly. They will do it in meetings where you aren't present or show in their remarks that they "are not with the program." Others will play the game and pretend that bygones are bygones, but that means that you are always going to have to watch for inconsistencies between what's coming out of their mouths and how they really behave. Do you really need this?

You may know an executive who is already in the company, and you may not think very highly of him. In all probability, he will know this, too, and be part of an "undercurrent" problem you experience with him because he will be concerned that you will readily replace him.

Hidden in Plain Sight

You will not be able to identify some of these people immediately. Observe and be patient, allowing them time to show themselves. It means you will have to experience their lack of loyalty, or let them produce a certain amount of toxic fumes which won't reach your nose immediately. But when they make their moves, or produce a constant low buzz of criticism to all who will hear, then you will have made your identification. You may even be surprised that one or several of these people may be part of your inner-circle management group, people with whom you previously had what you considered a good and positive working relationship.

Problems of Your Own Making

People who were neutral when you came into the company and have remained so during the first period of time may eventually turn against you if they feel you have pushed them too hard, in an operational sense; in their eyes, you have attacked them and their work. You will know this very quickly because there will most likely have been some hard words exchanged between you and these people at some point during this process.

In a sense, you created an enemy by simply doing your job—it's the way you did it or what you did that may have caused the problem.

In the previous section on external competition, you were urged to hit the road to connect with your customers' value judgment on your company. If you should be on the road a lot, another executive may decide that it's too much, and that you should be penalized. You may even have asked the other executive to run things during your absence. She comes to the conclusion that she can run the company as well as you, but in the office—where you should be more often. She may then put some punch behind that thinking by saying it publically to anyone who will listen while gathering her shadow cabinets of supporters and self-interested people. One of those people listening to this ego trip will undoubtedly be someone who will tell you everything.

Securing Help in Identifying the Candidates

Cultivate and rely on key listening posts in the company to keep you continually aware of what is going on in the company. These are not snitches or kiss-ups, but people who like you and what you are doing, who admire your policies and where you are taking the company.

During this time, you will no doubt be involved in installing people from the outside into key positions in the company. Independent of the subject at hand, you are going to need some key people who are part of *your* team, who you have hired, and who you have elevated to a new higher position of responsibility. There's nothing like a little thanks and moving careers along to promote loyalty.

People who are extremely happy that you have joined the company as, or have been promoted from within to CEO may be motivated to help you because they had been ignored or marginalized in the past. Many of these people are probably genuinely content in their work and have good hearts and solid characters. Maybe they feel as though your presence has given them a chance to finally make a good impression so they can go somewhere in the company. People who warn you about negative influences in the company should not be dismissed as gossips. They may have a strong sense of fairness and integrity and harbor a large portion of disdain for the backstabbing, the politics, and the games aimed at you, or at anyone, for that matter. They will serve as effective listening posts without a tainted or self-serving agenda. But they will also fulfill another and perhaps very helpful function for you: If they think it is good for the company, they will give you a reality check by blending into their information some honestly critical words concerning what you are doing or have done or plan to do. Listen carefully to these people. They mean well in both a big-picture as well as a personal way.

Up-and-coming professionals you bring into the company and put into lower echelon positions will probably be loyal to you as long as you mentor them and see that they, assuming good performance, progress well in the company. Particularly effective in this regard is taking one of their ideas and making it an official part of the company's way of doing business. They will often honor your mentoring and support by providing you with certain information they have picked up—again not because you have expressly asked them for it, but because they want, in some way, to protect you from any "harm" coming your way.

In all of this support you receive, do not feel compelled to reward people outright for their support and consideration. Listen to them, respect their motivation, and thank them—and with real feeling—in the name of the company and its future. Give them the sense that they are appreciated; let them feel that you know where your friends are.

Neutralizing the threats: Shutdown time.

Once you have identified and isolated the non-loyalists, then you have a number of alternatives available to solve your problem. Remember what this is all about when you take these actions: These people want you hurt, reeling, embarrassed, or gone.

So here are the steps you should follow.

- **Seek a dialogue.** You want to at least demonstrate that you are giving these people an honest chance to talk out their problems with you individually, in a private conversation. In talking to them personally, indicate that you understand and accept that they may have critical or justifiable thoughts on your appointment or your policies. Tell them what you have observed and have heard; search for the open and honest dialogue, which, in the majority of cases, you will not get from them. Give them an opportunity to explain themselves, and give them also an opportunity to consider the consequences of their activities and actions. They need to get the point: "There are consequences for everything, and we have a job to do here, so if you want to continue to be part of that job, then cease and desist." Then observe behavior going forward. Check in with your listening posts. If it is still apparent that the initial reasons for talking to these people continue to exist, then you should not repeat the process. They've had their chances.

- **Initiate the first steps of your termination strategy.** Those who step far, hard, and repeatedly over the line deserve it. And you don't need to harbor any doubts about what you are preparing to do. They have become a disruptive influence in the flow of the operational efficiency of the company and are creating tension and distraction among your top management. Ignore these disruptions, and your people's respect for you will decline rapidly. Such terminations are not going to work if all you have to show for it is a personal dislike for you as reason. You are going to have to study each individual case and design a program to eliminate the problem. You need serious job- and company-related reasons to give them, should they hypocritically ask for such detail as to why you have chosen to take this step. No matter how the whole situation plays out, make sure your board is briefed on your thoughts and your intentions. This action will involve very carefully studying your candidate's specific weaknesses, in addition to paying special attention to his meeting or not meeting certain agreed-upon performance goals. In addition, you might explore installing someone underneath the candidate who you have chosen as "coming management talent," and who possesses the qualifications necessary to succeed your candidate some day. This effectively opens up a second front beneath your candidate, with which he will have to contend. He will be kept busy watching his back, which will have the ancillary effect of taking some of the pressure off of you. It's one of the very effective ways to blunt/ neutralize any direct moves against you. If your candidate complains that you are interfering in his divisional affairs, tell him the person is too good to pass up and how thankful you are for his understanding, company loyalty, and for his acceptance of the person joining the department. He will understand the real message. And you? You are covered both ways: If your candidate continues to fight the situation in which he finds himself, then your decision is more than clear. If he works within the system and continues to do his job well, then he has accepted the status quo, and you still have a successor for him in place should he go back to his original ways at some point.

- **Shorten the termination preparation period.** If your opponent has some blowhard tendencies and is also not particularly well-versed in the ways of the press and the questions that are often asked, brief one of your (very) trustworthy journalist friends who calls you regularly asking about the company. When he does contact you, suggest that he call Joe Blow instead and ask him for a couple of quotes on current economic matters, as well as his views on the direction the company is taking. It is very likely that your candidate will be so full of himself at this recognition that he will go off into unfamiliar territory and say things regarding the company or its management that he will regret later when he sees them in printed form. Your risk, of course, is the fact that there is now an article containing "quoted" concerns about the company and its direction in the public domain. But then, you have your candidate where you want to have him. His regret, your advantage. The next press release would contain information on his departure from the company. Business people are good at putting two and two together. Translation: You took care of the problem.

- **Terminate the person.** Conduct a closed-door conversation with the person, discuss his performance, attitude, and the machinations you have observed. Drive the conversation to a point where it is clear to the person involved that a serious rupture in your relationship has taken place. Then you can deliver the words you have had in your head for weeks: "I think we should stop right there. I want to inform you that I have lost all confidence in your ability to conduct your duties in a manner that is positive and goal-oriented for this company.

We should seriously consider the alternative." The person involved doesn't need any lessons on what the word alternative imeans. Make the end happen then and there.

- **Check for metastasizing**. In all likelihood, the person involved wasn't operating alone. He possibly had an on-going support system of people who shared his opinions and wanted to bring you down. You started off playing hardball, now finish it with hardball. Speak to his department or division people about the change that has taken place. Despite your diplomacy in expressing your regret at his leaving, everyone will know what you are really saying. Some will move on and change; others will continue to foster hate. Eliminate any co-conspirators at the same time. Clear the table and get on with your job.

There is a degree of Machiavellian method in all of this. But this is reality. Sometime in the future, you could face these kinds of challenges. Use your power wisely and professionally, use it sparingly, and take your time. But when the moment has come to use it, use it with all consequence and with all directness. This is not a game in which it's fine for one team to win today and the other to win tomorrow. This is about your position and staying in that position to fulfill your duties. There is no Plan B here.

THE FAMILY FACTOR: WORKING WITH THE POWER OF BLOOD

Family-run companies have been pillars of entrepreneurism and models in their drive to attain a leading position in their respective markets. Founders have set visionary courses that have been followed and, in most cases, strengthened and broadened by the next generation. These companies gain huge forward momentum because their leaders have an abiding pride in family ownership, and an irrepressible belief that they will succeed in their efforts. Their drive is fueled by the family's deep desire to make a lasting imprint on business history, while the family itself gains fortune and fame in the process. This is determination that is entrenched deeply in the psyche of the family.

But what happens in a family company, or in a non-profit organization run by a cause-centered founding board, when a leadership vacuum has arisen, and where there may be no internal or family members qualified enough to fill it? Clearly, the reins of family or privately held companies are not easily loosened or shared, but there are times when there is no choice but to do so.

One can experience one set of challenges and expectations when a supposedly objective and profit-focused board does the hiring, but quite another when the board is family, or at least one dominated by family or private individuals. In the latter case, a more emotionally based decision has been made to search for an outside CEO, a tough and competent corporate-experienced executive, to run the company, but a very difficult emotional-based decision because it involves giving away some operational control on the part of the family, something they intend to do more out of necessity than out of conviction.

This is a company whose successes had been driven more by initial strong demand for a special set of products designed by the founder than by well-founded acumen and professionalism in managing the subsequent growth and positioning of the company. The leadership of the company is more or less rudderless and nepotism has not contributed to a crisp and professional execution to continue the company growth. Instead, a major downward trend has established itself in the last several years and a small measure of panic is in the air. The new CEO must restore the past brilliance and image of the company, but do it with new and different means going forward.

When a family takes the action of hiring an outsider, this decision can arise from a certain street-smart recognition that the company platform needs a stronger managerial hand than it is experiencing with its current management by family members. However, it may also come from major warning signs, such as broad-based quality issues or repeated and destructive production delays, customer complaints, or a decline in margins and correspondingly in profits. Or perhaps the family's trusted advisors or banks, seeking to protect their investment and the loans made to the company, may have pressed for a strengthening of the company's top management.

Whatever the reason, you are the result. After smiling your way through the congratulatory rounds, one fact is clear: You have entered an alien world. Your standard corporate experience may have prepared you for many things, but not something that approaches a relationship with business in-laws.

The first thing you are going to learn in your new "family" situation is that everything doesn't work like it did in your former world, even if that world of the past included working within another family company. Anyone who has been married more than once knows that every set of in-laws is different. Each private company has its own micro-culture, containing a distinct emotional makeup, relating both to the players and to their respective agendas. It is no secret that such factors can sometimes give rise to idiosyncratic business models and practices. There is a very strong pride factor involved in their thinking because they have built a company from scratch and have a strong track record. In fact, there are times when the word despotic would be a mild way of expressing how the company culture has evolved and the company has been led. But the methodology applied successfully in the past can be very different from the methodology they are going to need to continue that kind of performance.

A family-owned company is generally private in two ways. First, it is private in terms of legal classification. Second, it is private in the sense that it doesn't want analysts or the media peeking into its intimate affairs. "We do things our way" is often the mantra and the policy of the family. Who can blame them? If a family built a company with success factors that can be passed on from generation to generation, then the company has a long track record of doing what works. However, in relating to the rest of the corporate world, the family can have some "connection" difficulties that can seriously affect its ability to run and interact with that world.

Secondly, you will discover, surprisingly in some cases, that some of the important members of the family, even if they have been involved in the operational part of the business, may not understand a lot of the corporate-based language or methodology to which you are accustomed. They will, however, be looking for some of the buzz words, because that means the talent they have hired knows his or her stuff; they will want conceptual help as well as operational help. They will want to know that they are being "managed," but their definition of management and yours may be at odds, in spite of detailed discussions in this regard prior to your accepting their offer.

The description of the situation in the company, extensively discussed in both the formal as well as the evening or weekend sessions you had with the family during the recruiting process, could possibly deviate substantially from what you will find to be the case once you are installed as the chief executive and running "their" company. Their understanding of how much freedom they are willing to give to the new outside person to initiate needed changes may differ from your understanding of what you need in order to do your job. Therefore, clarity right up front, particularly relating to the scope of your decision-making ability, is of primary importance for both sides.

Thirdly, you are going to need to recognize the fact that, in a certain way, you have become their possession. Each family member will potentially look upon you as a personal route to getting whatever agenda she wants carried out or feels is appropriate to promote the growth of the company and its bank account. Family members will bombard you with their ideas and views on the company, how it should be managed, what one should do with a certain product, or with the niece, nephew, or cousin that somehow managed to get into a key position in the company. You will be called upon to be not only the driving managerial force behind the growth of the company, but also peacemaker, advisor, counselor, consultant, and magician.

Next, your diplomatic abilities will be tested in every imaginable way. You may even find yourself yelled at for the first time in your career. After all, if family members occasionally yell at each other, they have no reason not to yell at you, either. To add spice to this brew: You know already that you have entered into a world of great "prior" company success. But after several weeks in the company, you know that their view of the current situation and your view of the very same situation are very different. They have brought you into their company to make some changes and to get the company back to growing solidly again. But the situation in-house is worse than you thought. You are now faced with the additional burden of telling those family members, who think their company is simply in need of some improvements and better leadership, that this belief on their part is erroneous and misplaced. On top of that, money isn't going to flow like it has in the past.

You need a road map. You need to know how to protect yourself in this situation, and, at the same time, manage "your" family and their company in the most effective manner possible.

Establishing Your Modus Operandi: Do's and Don'ts

Before you begin work, sign an employment contract with the family, using your own independent legal counsel. The contract should define the entire standard employment contract items, including income, adjustment of same, and length of service. But that's not all. It should include a definition of procedures and steps relating to you or the family to exit the contract. The latter should, in particular, cover all financially related matters that would be involved in that eventual situation. The contract should have a length of at least three years and list your responsibilities, as well as those areas where, in spite of an official budget, you will need to seek family approval. You should also have spending limits included for the various disciplines of the company, such as marketing programs. Do not attempt to put too much detail into a listing of your operational responsibilities or the basic principles relating to your duties and obligations as the new CEO. Do list and get basic agreement on those you think are very important to run the company in the manner you deem necessary. However, you don't want to put too much detail into this because you don't want to confine yourself within too structured a framework. You will find yourself essentially carving out your path as you go along.

At the beginning of your tenure, you will possibly be put under pressure to quickly come up with the plan to move the company forward. Resist the impulse to accede to this wish and thereby show how good you are. Instead, you will want to spend at least three months studying and analyzing the company in its entirety, doing the classic analysis of the strengths, weaknesses, opportunities, and threats of the company, and then presenting your findings along with your initial recommendations to the family. This analysis will be the basis for many of your future proposals, so the time you must spend on this exercise is something they must understand and accept up front. Change is hard, and emotions and pride run high in a family company. There may be latent resentment if your approach is overly emotional or critical, or if you have found certain things that were deemed buried and forgotten, or should have been addressed in the past but wasn't. Meet before the presentation with the majority owner himself and make him aware, in detail, of your findings and what, based on those findings, you will propose the company should do. There should be no need to explain why this is necessary. Make sure, in individual follow-up discussions after the presentation meeting, that everyone in the family, as well as the members who are active in the company, understand completely, both in terms of strengths and weaknesses, where the company finds itself and what needs to be addressed going forward.

In your work aimed at securing the company's—and family's—future, be particularly aware of the strengths or weaknesses of the older products you may find in the company's current offering to the market. Often, family-run companies will hang on to products that have been good to them in the past, and not adapt to changing conditions in the market by dropping them for more current and attractive product. They may still be throwing money at the further development of these out-of-date products in the hope that, by improving them and their sales, they can help return the company to its former leadership position. You will know what you would like to say publicly about this kind of mindset. But the smarter move is to wait until you have a new money-making product line or two to show as a substitute for that to which they continue to cling.

As you advance your preparations for a new company product presence in the market, you will need to take them beyond this stubbornness, which could drag them into being tempted to repeat the same past errors instead of recreating the innovation and insight that launched the company. You will need to continue to challenge the family to repeat—from a creative point of view—what they did so successfully in the past, and you will need to reiterate and repeatedly emphasize the market-oriented ways that will allow them to attain that same success in the future. Involve them broadly and deeply in the new product development you are pushing forward.

Do not prepare huge slide presentations whenever you are making a proposal to family members. What will usually suffice is a succinct memo, an analysis of the critical success factors, a listing of critical assumptions in the proposal, and an appendix showing in clear, simple form the financial implications and results expected from the particular project. Do not make the mistake, in front of family members or other company personnel, of referring back to your earlier corporate life, or singing the praises of corporate structure and what that means for company success. You could very well generate resentment or feelings of inadequacy. Your arguments and convincing the company to move in a specific direction should be based upon your business analysis and substantive arguments, not because it worked somewhere else.

Do not make friends with any of the members of the family. You can expect to be invited to "welcome dinners" or the occasional party at their homes. Accept these invitations, but afterwards, keep your distance.

Do not take sides with a family member against other members of the family. Neutrality will be difficult to maintain, but it is the best and the only policy you can follow. You will be confronted often with this problem: A family member will come to you and complain about some other member of the family or discuss with you which flaws in the company result from that person's "poor" judgment. They may even put a detailed list of recommendations into your hands showing what needs to be done. The minute you start offering suggestions about the manner in which any of these issues can be resolved, you have put yourself into a compromising position. Cite your primary goal and that for which you were hired way back at the beginning. Maintain this independence, because the alternative is disaster.

Seek a close and collaborative relationship with the company CFO. In particular, you need to carefully watch the use of company funds, not only the sources of it. Cash or fund withdrawals by family members entitled to do so can cause unexpected difficulties, particularly when you are planning a major project, investment, or even paying normal bills at the same time. It is important that you have regular meetings with the active family members on this subject to avoid any unpleasantness, embarrassment, or the bad effects of a house purchase or loan to the family. Schedule regular finance committee meetings with the operational members of the family at least once a month and with the whole family, at least twice a year.

One of the very difficult things you will face is nepotism, which is a thorny problem because the family naturally has a desire to take care of its own. This can potentially represent a serious issue for you, because many times the family is not thinking of just any position for a fellow family member. They are talking about key positions that play an important role in organizational and operational planning. You will be asked to cooperate and to mentor the person "so we can see what he can really do." Refuse without rancor, but make sure, just in case the whole thing starts to go against you, that you have prepared a list of several alternative positions within the company where these people could potentially make a contribution. And make sure your proposal leads to the family's interests, otherwise you haven't a chance.

Work hard for the family. Be loyal. Show them you care for their concerns and worries. Listen to them and counsel them on business issues, where appropriate. When they share their concerns, even family-related ones, it is their way of reaching out to you and asking you for help. They will not explicitly ask for it, but the information or discussion they are conducting with you very clearly contains that request. Don't, however, forget the need for neutrality in all matters relating to internal family squabbles or situations.

Respect their business instincts, which seem to have been at least pretty good over a number of years, because otherwise there wouldn't be a company, and you wouldn't be there. But do not be obsequious in your daily dealings with them. You may "serve at their pleasure," but you don't serve them hand and foot, and say yes to everything they want.

Occasionally, there will be times when you will try to convince the family to take a series of steps which, if executed and financed properly, will lead the company from its present position to a more solid platform and higher financial return for the family. You are going to need support. Where are you going to find it? Even before you started with the company, and certainly after you have been there for several months, you should have identified the key *consiglieri* of the family, upon whose advice and counsel they have depended ever since the company was founded. Most often, you find such people among the legal and financial advisors of the company, as well as personal friends of the family who occasionally will come into the company for visits and is very clearly among those the family listens to very carefully. Don't even wait for a situation where you would need their immediate and positive support, but will court them over a long period of time by showing your respect for their position and their enormous contribution to the company over many years. Meet with them, take them into your confidence, inform them, ask for their opinion and views, and give them the satisfaction of seeing things they have suggested put into actual practice in the company. It is absolutely astounding how giving a little here and there will come back to you at other times when you really need it. You will show them continually that you respect and value their continued participation in strategic matters of the company. The smart ones—and they wouldn't be there if they weren't—know what is really going on. But they will play the game with you because it serves their purposes as well, including making sure that they get their monthly invoices paid at the end of each month.

None of these relationships with family advisors fundamentally weaken your position or your leadership. What it effectively does for you is very simple: You are then in a position to draw on their support and their long-term relationship with the family to do something you consider good for the family and the company, something you might, because of the magnitude of the change of direction or investment, not have been able to put through alone and have it accepted by the family.

When you are with the family, you will note that they fall into a pattern of conversation that reflects their style—direct or circuitous. Try not to violate the rules of the game. You are not family, but mix it up with them in the way they relate to one another.

In summary, working within a family-owned company can be an exhilarating and broadening experience. Nowhere else will you find such extremes, and nowhere else in the corporate world will you have such an opportunity to test your abilities as a manager, as a leader, and as a diplomat.

WORKING WITH THE BOARD: YOU NEED THEM MORE THAN THEY NEED YOU

You are quite aware of the fact that perception, reality, and level of expectations affect the nature of the way your board/owners will view you and your performance. You also know that the board members, from disparate backgrounds and with relatively limited time, generally have a difficult time understanding some of the more complex issues relating to the business you are running.

They also happen to be human. They have information comfort zones, levels of expectations, likes, and dislikes. They get frustrated and can lose patience, or forget what they have read or been told because they only saw it once in a 100-plus page briefing book. They are worried about being blindsided because of the depth and breadth of a business that probably stretches around the world. They are worried about their liability and reputations. They are also worried about the fact that they haven't direct and personal experience with many of the things they are being asked to consider and pass opinions on. Nonetheless, they have a stewardship function as it relates to the stakeholders of the company; they are your boss.

At issue here is your relationship with the board and how you should approach making it a successful and mutually beneficial one. You may have known some of the members of the board before you took on the position, which makes your current task a somewhat less formal one, but only because you and they have a personal relationship, which is not to be confused with the business relationship it has now become. Boards and their makeup and duties conform to the specific company situation and its current stage of development. Board meetings are conducted differently depending upon whether the board has strategic oversight of an early stage start-up, or oversees a Fortune 500 company. No matter the size or the individual situation of the company, the essential duties and responsibilities are the same.

So what are the things you should be concentrating on or doing when you think "board?" The essence of your relationship with the board can be summarized in several key questions:

- Does the board understand what you and the company are doing as well as planning to do?
- Does it consider the growth strategy or strategies (business plans and business model) behind these activities to be appropriate and financially sound?
- Does it consider that all recognizable and identifiable risks are being appropriately managed or held in check?
- Does it believe that the management team in place is entirely capable of executing its plans and, at the same time, minimizing the risks involved?
- Does it believe that the business of the company is being conducted in a forthright and correct fashion and that practice of integrity in the company's operations is the measure of all things?
- Does it believe that you are the right person for the job you hold?

Ongoing complete and satisfactory answers to these questions depend upon the common thread of the overall relationship: continuous communication and dialogue initiated and maintained by both parties. So how does the board get all the information it needs to fulfill its obligation? Are there dangers involved in misrepresented or incomplete information flowing to the board? Do the board members differentiate between what they think they see and what really is? And how do you influence all of this? One thing is clear: If you are not the major influence in shaping their perceptions and expectations of your—and your company's—operational progress, or you are not particularly good at political chess, then you have a problem.

Secondly, being the major influence in shaping board perceptions does not mean that you attempt to shut down any other sources of information the board may wish to consult. You couldn't anyway because part of the board's job is to be well-acquainted with your team, its functions, and problems and conflicts. They will want to get this information directly. And you have always maintained that you run an open shop, haven't you? You want the board to have the feeling it can talk to your people and meet with them whenever they feel it necessary. If you have chosen your team well and they are professionals, and you have been informing the board about any and all problems in the company, then there is nothing that they don't already know.

The danger in all of this lies perhaps more in the area of partially unintended (or intended) inaccurate information being passed to the board. You speak constantly with your top management, so they theoretically are on top of every issue facing the company, as well as those parts of the operation that are doing well. Nonetheless, one of the ways you can neutralize inaccuracy or something falling off the cliff is to dialogue, in detail, with your top management on the content of the information, both formal and informal, that is to be sent, provided, or discussed with board members. Your team needs to understand thoroughly what the exact current status of the company is. Thus, when such information is shared with the board, both formally and informally, that information is always consistently accurate. This is not censorship, but it does have the effect of putting some very effective balance and consensus into the information flow, whatever the situation or whatever the issues or problems in the company may be. And it is an effective way for you to have major influence as well as a balanced measure of control over the information reaching or being discussed with the board. In addition, because the information flowing to the board reflects the true situation of the company at all times, you won't be getting any calls referencing possible "misinformation" flowing to the board, which you would have to justify or explain.

Thirdly, you started off your tenure by meeting individually with each and every board member before you even moved into your office. Periodically, you have made it a point to spend quality time with the individual board members (the independent members of the board in particular) to give them a balanced and realistic picture of the company and its progress. This is smart, productive, and effective "board relationship"cultivation, which you should continually practice during your tenure as CEO.

The more you personally and frequently inform, the more you discuss with your board, the more you show respect for their functions and responsibilities, the more they will know that you take them seriously. The result should be the continued existence of a rolling consensus from your board for your management of the company and for your strategy.

In short, always keep the board members informed in real-time about where you are taking the company. And with that supporting wind at your back, you can continue to maintain your current heading.

WHO'S THAT STANDING IN OUR WAY? UH-OH. IT'S US.

Whenever a serious problem affecting a company's fortunes arises, those involved will generally start to look first for the external factors, which, in all probability, caused the bad situation. In addition, they might mix in a fleeting "we blew it, too" statement into any explanation, just to keep things more or less honest. No question, it is not easy to admit culpability. But too often, the reasons given are skewed more to the external factors than to any internal issues that could have been the *real* problem. Their thinking is, "Great big world out there, folks. Lots of places to look for reasons why some project or product launch didn't work the way it should have."

It is astounding to see to what lengths people will go to redirect or to deflect criticism from their own personal failings. Or, in the case of company operations, from bad internal communication, unclear lines of authority, haphazard use of financial controls, delayed product development, sloppy planning or execution, or constant misreading of the market and its needs. These are the dangerous, top-tier problems, the ongoing problems everyone in the company knows exist, but about which little or nothing has ever been done to mitigate or eliminate their negative influence. Instead, the guilty party is more likely external. "The market won't bend to our will. There's not much we can do about that."

This is a recipe for second-class company performance and, longer term, perhaps even loss of the company.

One example of a dangerous problem took place years ago in an American company with subsidiary sales operations in Europe and the Middle East. In a fit of frustration at outside vendor product quality problems, the company decided to design and produce the part itself. Here are the scenes from this unfortunate event:

- The company had no former experience in developing this part.
- The company used one particular set of regulatory standards in the design of the part, making it difficult to install in countries accustomed to a different method of installation and technical specification.
- Convinced that it had a solution to the problem, the company proceeded with production and delivery of the part.

Major problems in the form of returns, as well as higher costs and warranty problems struck immediately. But it took months for the company to admit that it wasn't the incompetence of customers installing the product in the field. Instead, it had been the company's own design and internally generated false assumptions that had caused the problem.

Here is another example of this kind of thinking. Consider the comments of the sales personnel of a French company. When sales didn't increase according to plan, but purchasing had already brought in parts in order to produce to that plan, a witch hunt began. The management of the purchasing department accused the sales force of incompetence and laziness. That wasn't completely inappropriate in this case; performance was an issue. However, instead of the sales force admitting they had misjudged the market in their budgets again, they cited a number of colorful external reasons why those budgeted sales had not been achieved: weather, the economy, change in customer tastes, order postponements, miscellaneous bad stuff happening with shipments to customers. All their reasons shifted the blame elsewhere. Internal problems were wholly absent from the list of reasons.

In contrast, consider the sales professionals of a British company who also had a "sales" problem. The market wasn't in the best shape that year. Budgeted sales were much too high. Nevertheless, the sales professionals repeated what they had told management many times before. They maintained that certain products were too expensive, they were too complicated to install, and too many of the products fell short in reliability because of limited user/ market testing.

They pointed the finger at problems within the company, all of them the result of fundamental internal deficits, including hubris, stubbornness, and product development done more for the sake of showing technical expertise than in the interest of the customer. Problematic at best was management's attitudinal approach to product pricing: "We will set the customer sales price when we have all the costs."

Unfortunately, despite the repeated honesty and concerns of the sales team, the company didn't react. There was almost no detailed follow-up analysis of the internal phases of the product's development, no realization that production, purchasing, and sales/marketing should have been involved from the start in the development process, including setting an appropriate and binding initial target price for the product. There was no recognition that mistakes in the design had been made, driving costs too high, no admission that the product had perhaps been overdeveloped for the relevant market needs.

Instead, management showed its frustration by looking for external reasons: raw material cost increases. Customers don't appreciate quality when they see it. Unexpected changes in customer tastes and needs. Of course, the sales force got some flak as well. But overall, external reasons were the main cause of the problem.

There are also other factors that can play a role in a company continuing to run away from the truth. Whether or not the CEO will admit it, she may very well know the *real* reasons why the program or project failed to live up to expectations. But the culture of the company makes generous allowances for the inclusion of external issues or problems. In such a company, management is often quite convinced they are doing the right thing at all times.

In addition, some CEOs react emotionally to any hint of internal problems being the cause, most likely because they interpret any acknowledgement of the enemy within as being a sign of their failure in leading the company. Their sensitivities and their egos stand in the way of intellectually coming to grips with the problem. They think, "I know there are internal issues, but all of that is already being taken care of, and we are on the right road to solving our problems." If the CEO is guilty of this thinking, then where are the mindsets of the other people in the company?

What does this mean for the smart CEO? If you happen to be a CEO of a company who is ignoring internal problems, if you refuse to look for the real ownership of the problems that are damaging your company and its success, if you like short-term "fixes", then, in all likelihood, you will not be leading your company much longer. Neither management, nor a company can survive when they continually operate in the denial zone.

If you are a CEO who is new to the company, or you have had a much needed basic revelation about what *really* needs to be done in your company, then here is the smart way to proceed.

Listen carefully to those honest and realistic souls in your company who live in a world of frustration due to internal problems. Theirs is a world of anger that possibly looks at your company, and your performance, and sees what it could be, but isn't. Theirs is a world that has most likely been marred by prior superficial acknowledgment of the problems followed by repeated "we will do better" actions that went nowhere. Ever wonder why you have lost good people to the competition or to other industries? The reason could be under your nose. Very possibly, your company has not recognized the enemy within, but your former employees saw that enemy and ran for their lives.

The smart CEO will listen only to *substantive* external reasons, and then evaluate their relevance. She will assign some probability and value to them, and want to check if there couldn't be a better way of anticipating such problems or hindrances in advance. She will want to recheck the critical assumptions relating to any relevant external factors to make sure they had been adequately considered and built right from the start into any forecasts or budgets the company may be currently using.

Following this analysis, the CEO will turn his attention inward to self-inflicted internal blockages. In doing this, first of all you must remember that you and/or your top management have a credibility problem: Internal problems and their dangers have been around in the company for quite a while. Many of your good people may have already left or "quit" inside because of them, so you are essentially dealing with those who, for reasons of inertia or for personal reasons, stayed with the company in spite of its second-class performance. While your people may have heard some of the same songs of intent in the past, they will still have the hope and the need to see proof that management really means what it says this time.

You should start with a clear and honest statement: The real enemy is *our* incompetence and *our* inability to do our jobs in a correct and continuously reliable market-oriented fashion. You will further your intention to put together, *with your employees' help*, a complete list of internal problems that are adversely affecting the fortunes of the company. You don't need to spend enormous amounts of time on this exercise, because the *problems are already well-known*. You will further announce your intention to focus relevant and adequate resources on finding a solution for, and thereby resolving, two or three of the most serious problems you and your people have identified. Continue to focus your and the company's efforts on these problems until they no longer exist. This will include regular review sessions involving detailed discussions of the steps agreed upon to solve the individual problem and the progress achieved toward elimination of the problem. Your people have heard enough words. Only credible, focused, and *continued* action will suffice to prove to them that the company management has serious and long-term intentions to resolve its internal problems.

No question: The exercise of eliminating the enemy within is your highest priority. A situation of this sort strikes at the heart of the operational integrity of a company. It shows a company weak at its center and ill-prepared to win a competitive war of any sort in the market. In a well-run company, both the internal and external problems are seen as one and the same. Attempting to minimize or rationalize serious internal problems solves nothing.

WHY THEM, NOT US? YOUR FAIR SHARE DOESN'T HAVE TO BE WHAT YOUR CUSTOMER THINKS IT SHOULD BE

You think you know all about the competition. You have a high degree of confidence in how your products or services rate in comparison, and that you know the relative market shares of your respective companies, their distribution policies, their sales conditions, and their relative financial strength. You even have a fairly good handle on their new product development. Yet with all the information, one key bit is missing: Why does the competition often seem to be gaining the upper hand? Even existing customers aren't buying more from you. Both your subjective and objective information indicate your company is competitive and respected, and that your brand is well-known. Your company is bringing new product to the marketplace on a frequent basis. But sales are just barely ahead of last year's, and profits are lagging. You wonder, *What am I missing here?*

Former U.S. Secretary of Defense Donald Rumsfeld observed in a 2002 Department briefing, there are known knowns, known unknowns, and unknown unknowns.

The known knowns are the results of your standard comparisons of all the usual suspects:

- Individual product comparisons with comparative strengths and weaknesses
- Product line balance with all relevant market-based price points "spoken to"
- Selling terms and conditions
- Application of the terms of conditions in daily sales operations
- Product distribution policies
- Customer comparison metrics
- Frequency and effectiveness of sales calls
- Involvement of senior sales management in the field as well as the effectiveness of their visits
- Delivery contracts
- Advertising and promotions
- Customer aggressiveness in pricing and promotional offers

- Cumulative history of company and competitive prices increases and manner of execution
- Website effectiveness (hits and page impressions) using SEO
- Delivery scheduling including on-time delivery and product availability metrics
- Product quality benchmarks
- Merchandising (if appropriate) in customer service
- Type of and frequency of customer calls
- Turn-around time for customer credits
- Return and service policies and effectiveness of same
- Potential recalls
- Packing and packaging, including multi-language instructions and useful hints for the customer
- Consumer research

In a word, just about everything that can be quantified as well as described.

Without a doubt, an analysis of the knowns will result in a number of things you are already working on, and perhaps a thing or two that you and your people feel have been missing in the total mix of product, product presentation, and sale to your customers. But otherwise, things look pretty good. The comparisons appear to give your company the edge. But you still have a vague feeling something is wrong.

Welcome to the worlds of the known unknowns and unknown unknowns. The first category is the relevant information about product and service that your customers and prospects have not discussed or have not been asked to discuss with your sales team, market analysts, or consultants. The second category refers to other facts, value judgments, and internal problems relating to your company and its performance that only your customers and prospects know and are most likely using against you. They aren't even on your checklists or datasheets; they never occurred to you.

In analyzing the comparative information produced by your sales and marketing people, there doesn't seem to be much difference between your whole product and marketing approach and that of the competition. Look at the list again: It goes on and on, but no relative value has been assigned to each of the items on the checklist. This makes it very difficult to assign degrees of relative importance to these points. In addition, you notice that some of the less quantifiable elements of the customer relationship are not even on the list—like moral responsibility to the customer when something goes wrong. Do you really know what your customers value, and what specific things on that list are more important to them than others? Supplementing these kinds of comparisons with that information and analysis shouldn't be the most difficult task you have given your sales and marketing people.

What should you do about the unknown unknowns? Sometimes delegation of responsibilities has definite drawbacks. Your marketing department provides you with all kinds of reports on how the company and its product or services compare to the competition, but does this information really give you the answer as to why your customers are not all buying up to their potential? Although your top sales management team will naturally be included in this exercise, the answer is you—the best person to take the lead on addressing the unknown unknowns and finding out what they really are.

To do this, you are not going to go to your customer's purchasing manager or one of their production people and ask, "Why them, not us?" They are most likely not where you are going to find the real, possibly buried, answers you are seeking. You might hear issues relating to your prices, terms, or something about a quality problem on the last shipment, but nothing more sophisticated than that.

You need to look for the *value judgment* that has been made on your company, the hidden reasons why your customer's relationship with your company is perhaps only tenuous, and why your customer is buying more from the competition than your company. You are looking for the reasons why your value proposition, well-accepted by some of your customers, isn't coming across to other customers in the same way. The fact is that you are most likely not going to find the real reasons at the third or fourth level of your customer's organization, or detailed in a report from one of your salespeople referencing a discussion he had with a buyer.

So, with some doubt in your mind as to the efficacy of this exercise, you start to visit several of your counterpart CEOs or owners. Assuming you have introduced the subject on the phone before your visit, you may find that your colleague either has a clear opinion on your company and its products, or has gone to the trouble to put together reasons why his company's purchase volume has sunk. These reasons will most definitely give you some new insights into the mindset of your customer. Your colleague may express his appreciation at having the opportunity to speak with you about some real problems from the past that were either badly resolved, or have not yet been resolved. You may also learn why he considers your product not as competitive for his purposes as those of your competition. Or your colleague may give you up a very personal reason for his company not buying. Now you are really listening. For example, perhaps he's heard something negative about your company, or personally experienced negative issues that had hurt his standing and reputation within his company. The latter is obviously the more serious of the two and you can be sure he expressed his displeasure or reservations about your product or services to any and all who would listen.

Whatever your visit turns up, you will finally have something you can deal with. You will have a set of specific reasons and problems to consider and rectify, and you will have first-class information about the value that has been placed on your products, the relationship, or the conduct of business between your company and your customer.

Your colleague will appreciate your visit, particularly if he intends to remain a customer of yours. He will also be appreciative because he has finally had an opportunity to unload his feelings and position on the matter to someone from your company who can fix the problems. He knows you will take the information and views he has provided seriously and that you will take action. As a result, some of the unknown unknowns have now become known knowns. Remember that this is not a one-time exercise. Visits such as these need to be high on your priority list as you move your company forward. A side benefit for you and your company is that you establish direct lines of communication to your colleagues in your customer's companies. They could be useful for other situations some day. Take care that you continuously manage and nurture these relationships.

OTHERS MAY, BUT WE DON'T DO THINGS THAT WAY: CULTURE TRUMPS CULT

Your power to make things happen is something you enjoy and practice with a steady hand. But there are also times when company culture can dominate, influence, and create impact, good or bad, well beyond permissible limits.

Every company has "grown up" in a certain way. It has created its own culture along the way, often originating in how the founders spelled out a vision, set the direction of the company, and established the growth pattern that placed the company on the road to its present position. Over the years, the company culture was also affected by how that growth took place, for example, which customers were attracted to its products or services, the rate at which the company expanded, and the industry environment or niche economies in which it operated. In many cases, the particular culture of the company often resulted in a cloning effect. People who had similar or the same style or views gravitated to this company just as those already working for the company preferred, consciously or unconsciously, to hire those who were also "one of them."

Corporate culture is often visible. It can be seen in the company's devotion to the arts, the dress and manner of its people, the style of offices and their layout, the lifestyle weight room, the style of the architecture of its corporate headquarters, the food offered in the cafeteria or dining room, where the executives of the company have their offices, the aesthetics of the company product, the letters of congratulations and photos of management spread out for all to see, the cleanliness and polish of the factory floor, and the company car policy.

Company culture can also surface in spoken and written words. For example, the content of the company's mission statement, how management interacts with the press, its written information and hiring policies, the receptionist greeting or the telephone call center statements (in or out of country), the spoken judgment of its customers, its advertising, its CEO speaking at a public events, and the positioning and relative weighting of company-held values and their order of appearance in any of published statements or interviews.

Company culture can also be determined by what the company does within its confines or what activities it generates in its industry, the community, or the economy at large. Take a look at company-sponsored social activities, what philanthropic activities the company supports, and which community activities the company encourages its people to pursue when they have time to do so. Is inside-the-company weekend socializing part of the mantra of the culture, or is it frowned upon?

Another set of indicators of company culture relate to the company's operational activities and thinking about:

- how fast the company can or will develop product.
- how the organization is structured in terms of the number of reports each manager has.
- the size of the meetings and their structure.
- the manner in which information is disseminated.
- the number of confidential categories that are attached to internal documents or memos.
- the number of legal cases in which the company is involved and the publicity surrounding those cases.
- the rewards and compensation structure for the employees of the company.
- the care of and service to its customers.
- its openness or lack-thereof to internationalization of its business.
- its policies in each respective country in which it operates.
- its business practices in "border-line" cases.
- its risk orientation in terms of growth and investment.
- frequency and volume of company personnel fluctuation.
- the company's attitude toward laws and regulations directly affecting its business.

There can be "bad" company culture because of the human factor, that is, how the company operates toward its people and others with whom it comes into contact. Is there so much misplaced pride in a particular company culture that an individual gets compressed into the whole with no one checking to see if the person is really along for the whole trip? Yes, because the culture can cause a company to set itself apart, or beyond the reach of the normal mores of our society, including the laws and regulations that govern it and all who are part of it. That culture can sometimes approach holier-than-thou status, particularly when steered by arrogant people. This is a company culture approaching cult status.

Thankfully, however, company culture usually works the other way. It is often the positive and electrifying element in spurring and achieving success. In essence, it is the "chemical" interaction of enthusiastic and positive people interacting with and respecting one another in their efforts to grow the company. It is the tasks and bonding they have shared over years of working together for common goals, and a shared mindset. It is the way they relate to and interact with one another. It is the way they approach setting and then reaching the goals of the company. All these factors contribute to fueling a unique cultural motor that has the potential to drive that company forward.

Is it possible to effect major changes in a specific and already set culture? Consider this example. Let's assume that you have just been hired as CEO of a hot, growing company. This is not an early-stage company in incubation, but a maturing company with low nine-figure sales numbers. Your job is to guide this company toward greater success. You know exactly what you believe in, and where you want that company to go. At your level, you better have some hard-nosed principles because you are going to need them.

You have talked to other people who know the company and its workings well. The person who recruited you or convinced you that this was the right career step and the right challenge has made all the right noises about "great people and culture" waiting for you when you join the company. In fact, you have experienced most of that positivity in your interviews with the company.

But six months later, you have identified at least five or six major areas of cultural dissonance: Your cultural and philosophical approach, as well as the culture needed to drive the company forward, do not match up with the existing company culture. These areas represent potential blocks of further company progress. You conclude that certain parts of the current company culture need redirection and adjustment.

This is heavy stuff. You have specifically honed in on a number of cultural characteristics of the company that you believe will, if left unchanged, give competition a chance to forge ahead of you in the market. Examples might include very loose working hours, the manner in which the company is paying its best people, the company's hubris-filled approach to customer and economy, and the way the company approaches its new product development. Whatever it is, you recognize that this is part of the cultural status quo. You acknowledge that the first thing you will hear, should you attempt to change any of this, is, "We've always done it that way."

Nevertheless, you have decided to take action. There is just one small problem standing in your way: The very things you have chosen to change or eliminate or influence are a part of the central underpinnings of the company culture. They are baked hard into the air and the concrete of the company. Any shaking of these parts of the culture tree could result in something crashing down on your head.

Battle lines will form when people sense change is coming. You can almost hear the well-intentioned warning message from one of the directors, even if the change is clearly necessary: "We have done well with it that way. Why the change now?"

As you approach the change, first be clear that this is not about a business model change. Company culture revolves more around the soul of the organization; much like a human being. It has a personality, character, philosophy, behavior patterns, and idiosyncrasies. In addition, keep in mind there is no one "fix-it" tool for every company cultural change. Each individual situation requires creativity and understanding of all of the ramifications of any potential change. Every one of these situations will be different, with different weightings and problems, and therefore require a customized solution.

You know you are going to need to effect several major changes in the company culture in the coming months and years. If you handle it properly at the outset, you will set the stage for bigger, necessary changes.

Let's imagine a specific example: change in the working hours of the company. Up to this point in time, there has been essentially no real control whatsoever over the hours worked by your employees, even though policies on the matter exist. This is the way the company started off and grew; it's the "spirit and soul of our company." At the beginning of your tenure, you regarded all of this in a somewhat bemused fashion, but then it increasingly became a problem for you. People couldn't be found; meetings could only take place after all of the required "spirits" on the lawns and in the halls and exercise rooms had been rounded up. Preparedness for such meetings was often sketchy at best. Efficiency and organizational focus suffered.

And then the really serious part: At the moment, you may be the market leader, but the competition, also increasing in numbers, is getting better and better. They are focused, organized, and motivated, and their latest product launches signal mid-term danger for your company. Time to fix whatever it is that is flowing through the company's veins and weakening key parts of the body. The first step in this direction needs to be a mini-change involving curbing some of the problems and excesses of the "easy" work culture.

Have a serious chat with your HR vice president to explore the existing policies and what can be done to eliminate some of the negatives of the working hour situation. This is more of a formality than a practical solution. She will send out an e-mail reminding everyone of the need to respect the current working hour policies. Effect: zero. This doesn't change anyone's mind one bit. You embark on a campaign to win the hearts and minds of your directors and managers because you need them to understand the consequences of the current cultural policy for the company, their jobs, their stock options, and the growth of the company.

You give them the message in clear terms: Out there in the dark marketplace are several companies that want to take all of our present happy circumstances away from us. And they have already started doing it very successfully. You don't have to list all the consequences; give your people credit for being smart enough to know what your words and your action mean. They will march with you—and they will have no choice. Self-interest and interest in keeping the company success going will supersede giving up a cultural perk. A final plus for you: This kind of argument will be just as effective when you approach the problem of initiating other changes in the culture that will prevent or impede future company success.

Here's the beauty of it all. If you had just said, "I want this change in working hours because this sort of thing makes for sloppy operational execution, it is dangerous for the company, and it personally offends me," what do you think would have been the reaction of the company managers? A shrug or a dutiful nod, but no buy-in.

After ensuring that you have your management's support, have your HR dDepartment draw up the final, revised, still somewhat "loose" order of the day for the company working hours. Loose means you haven't reversed everything in the old policy, but certainly enough to make the new policy fit your plans for tighter and more focused working hours. Your top and middle managers will discuss the relevant details with your employees to make sure that everyone is on the same side of the street. You aren't done yet, though.

There may be certain employees—not just the free spirits, but people with families, or medical situations in the family who have built their life rhythm around the current working hours—who will have to or want to leave immediately. Pay particular attention to these and any other issues arising from the change. Do not make the mistake of leaving this problem on the table without your personal attention to it. This is the fair and human thing to do. Don't make the change a one-way , even if it is in the company's overall interests, as well as contributes to everyone's future job security. Take care of your people and their individual needs. Bend a little here and there, even if some will try to use that to their own advantage.

Key Priorities

- Your competition is not only outside of your company. There are people inside the company who want you neutralized or gone. Identify who they are, give them one chance, and then neutralize *them*.
- Working for a family company is not your typical corporate situation. It involves tact, diplomacy, patience, and subtle use of your abilities. It also involves you remaining who *you* are while, at the same time, working intensively with your new "in-laws" to change a little bit of who *they* are.
- You know exactly the role and the responsibilities of your board. And you have a good relationship with its members. Nevertheless, you run the company in the fashion you feel appropriate. How to link your independence and their role of strategic oversight in a positive way is a matter of communication and cooperation.
- External reasons for missing performance benchmarks are always easy to find. The *real* reasons are often internal. Even though culpability is not the easiest thing to admit to, you need to face this

situation by not only attacking the reasons for the bad numbers one by one, but also by making your recognition of their existence and their need for elimination credible.

- Your sales and margins are not where they should be, but you think your company has its best product or service lineup ever. Your fair share of the market isn't happening. There's very possibly a negative value judgment standing in your way and you personally need to get on the road to find out why your customers continue to apply that judgment in their buying decisions.

- Company cultures have a life of their own. They can be advantageous and they can be disadvantageous for your company—and for your plans to grow its business. Changes in those cultural attributes of your company are not accomplished in broad-based frontal attacks. You need to be subtle and you need to concentrate on a succession of mini-successes in any changes you might want to make.

Chapter 6

DIFFICULT SITUATIONS, DIFFICULT CHOICES

Just because you smile a lot and are friendly to all concerned doesn't mean that you are feeling the same way on the inside. Everyone will tell you that the job of CEO is a lonely one. Some will tell you that not every CEO who is one should be one. Stress, continual worry, and misplaced dreams of glory are not your friends. They can take you down the wrong paths, or lead you into saying things you never thought you would. Read about meanness, bad passion, doubt, and misdirected enthusiasm—and prescriptions not only for the symptoms, but also for the causes.

GOING OVER THE DARK LINE: TOUGHNESS VERSUS MEANNESS

There was a time in the United States when a leading business magazine annually published a list of the 10 toughest managers in the country. Being tough within the constraints of a leadership role is still a major attribute of successful CEOs today, and rightly so. But there

131

are limits to being tough because toughness has a counterpart called meanness. A tough manager thinks in a positive manner about the "us" factor—the
company, its employees, and its goals. A mean manager thinks about himself
and wants to hurt others to assuage his own turmoil.

The difference between toughness and meanness is a very fine line, not
easily identifiable in many cases. Cross that line, and you're hurting those
around you, as well as yourself, perhaps even fatally, in the professional sense.
There is nothing wrong with occasionally barking a bit, putting an ambitious
goal on the table, or conducting a critical performance appraisal when necessary. This kind of toughness, this kind of personal authenticity, oriented
toward driving the organization forward, is always recognized as useful.
Everyone understands it and accepts it. In many of its forms, it is the way you
must be in order to do your job effectively.

From another perspective, toughness implies the internalized ability and
willingness to be vulnerable, while meanness means one is actually uncomfortable being vulnerable and showing it. However, when you are tough, does
this necessarily imply that you can be mean at the same time, or are these
behavior patterns mutually exclusive? What kind of behavior keeps the CEO
tough and purposeful in his approach to the company, its goals, and its people, but does not have him going over the line and becoming a mean person?

Many years ago, I was recruited by the Vice CEO to join a major company in the consumer non-durables business. The man I reported to was the
same one whom I had known earlier in another company for which we had
both worked. This man had been and continued to be my mentor during this
time. I admired him and was loyal to him.

He was a tough and professional manager when he was the CEO of his
previous company. He was respected, experienced, caring, fair to a fault, direct, clear in his thinking, and respectful of peoples' feelings. He possessed
social graces, was clear in the goals he had established for the company, and
had a listening ear and observing eye. He was a motivator and a best-of-the-
best manager. When he walked into a meeting room, people stood up. When
he met one-on-one with someone, it was not, as the Germans say, *von oben
herab* (looking down on the person with whom he was speaking); he met
everyone from janitor to director on an equal plane. People felt that respect

and respected him for it. And when he rose to speak in a large meeting, there wasn't a sound in the hall. Everyone knew there were going to be some tough messages mixed in during his speech.

He often had hard words of criticism relative to various aspects of the company performance, but all of this was done in a manner that didn't hurt or denigrate people. Instead, it made everyone want to go out and correct what had gone wrong. They felt sorry for the fact that they had not performed up to his standards.

This man had an inner peace and didn't harbor ill feelings, hatred, or mockery. He knew who he was, his self-respect and identity were intact, and he liked people and liked working with them. If he had any frustrations, then he didn't reveal them, but worked through them himself. It was not his style to take them out on others, using language that would hurt or humiliate. And even though he may have felt it, he never used words publicly to imply that anyone or any ideas were stupid or inept. If there was something to be said, he did it one-on-one, behind closed doors.

He often said, "When I drive to work in the morning, I am always looking forward to seeing my colleagues again and working with them during the day." What an attitude! This man knew who he was; his feeling of self-worth was strong. It was a pleasure to hear him occasionally tell some stories about himself, a certain sign that he was confident in himself. Another important sign of his inner strength was his control and steadiness in dealing with various sticky or sensitive situations. Not a single person in the company was cowed by his presence, or so beaten down by him that they would not dare to utter criticism or propose a different way of doing things. His orientation was outward to the objectives and results of the company and showed his deeply felt sense of responsibility toward the owners and the success of the company.

After several years, we found ourselves working together again, this time in a turnaround situation involving lost market position, an ineffectual company organization, and heavy losses. For the first year, he was as I had known him in the previous years. The turnaround was taking place, losses had been reduced, and sales were starting to climb. But then he changed.

For the first time, I observed doubts and tentativeness in his manner, and erratic behavior in his treatment of colleagues and company personnel. He publicly berated employees and used his position to ride roughshod over any opposition. His body language was tense. What had caused this transformation? In spite of a number of the improvements in the company position, the company was still in a rough position and had just been sold to another company in Germany. He was under pressure, and the stress was starting to take its toll. The dark side, the mean side—which exists in all of us, sometimes latent, sometimes for all to see—had begun to work its way into his behavior and attitude. He started to strike out at everything around him to release the pressure he felt inside, but the relief from that internal pressure was only temporary. As the spiral within him accelerated, he became meaner to those around him.

Because I knew him well and felt I had his confidence, I shared my concerns with him, but he maintained that it was nothing. Sitting there, looking at him, I knew he was still the same as always, still the same man, and same competent executive he had always been. But, on one basic point, he wasn't. Unfortunately, he could not see himself as others were experiencing him.

One Sunday afternoon, he came to my home. During that visit, he took me aside and asked me why he was having so much difficulty getting people in the company to perform effectively; he suspected there was a feeling of disrespect for him. He even cited several instances where he felt that he had stepped over the line. I gave it to him straight out: "Once upon a time you were a tough manager. Now you have become a mean one." He nodded.

I told him that he had begun to unleash his inner frustration, his inner hate of his situation, and difficulty in solving company problems on others. I told him that this was not helping him, but hurting him massively; he had turned inwards and was using such behavior to assuage his inner turmoil. For his sake and the employees' sake, I encouraged him to sit down and do some serious introspection. I promised him I would draw his attention to instances of this sort in the future when I observed them. He was still my guy, still the very competent manger, but his emotional universe had turned upside down. His reaction to all of this was a sad smile.

After that afternoon, I sat and thought about him and the subject in general. Certain things appeared clear to me. Once that line between toughness and meanness is crossed, and a person has let those inner emotions overwhelm him, once the temporary feeling of release from an outward explosion provides the required internal rush, it then becomes extremely difficult or even impossible to turn around and return to the toughness side of the equation. The chains are almost too tight and the pattern too entrenched for toughness alone to offer the needed release from stress and trouble. My mentor and friend had become like Darth Vader, a prisoner of the demons that drove him.

What must a CEO do to manage his emotions intelligently and effectively when dealing with stress? If he happens to be in the denial phase—*I am doing nothing wrong; it's my people that have started to make more mistakes*—then he is definitely headed for a no-solution situation. His attitude blocks any possible healing.

What can you do to fight against this unhappy condition and thereby try to return to the zone of tough, mature leadership?

1. **Look inside yourself.** Just as you analyze the company's strengths and weaknesses, you must do the same thing with yourself. Be vigilant in observing yourself and what you do in stressful situations. Write down what happens—and don't kid yourself. Denial is a trap precluding the possibility of change. *This can't be me*, you think. But it is. And if you don't know what you have just done, but see the effects, then back up and analyze each situation for what caused it and why you felt that way. This is where your maturity and toughness with *yourself* come into play.

2. **Go where the loyalty is.** Perhaps most importantly, you are going to need loyal people in whom you can confide in and ask for help. You need them to observe you carefully and continuously, and to counsel you when you cross that line. This can, of course, be your spouse, but because this person is outside of the company, such observations on his or her part may be only marginally relevant. What you really need are sit-downs with a few of your most loyal colleagues in the company. Push them to give you their honest opinion. They are there and usually just waiting to help you.

3. **Professional help required.** If all else fails, get professional help. It can be problematic and time-consuming, but it may be your

best hope in the long run. An executive coach can provide help on honing people skills; a psychologist can help you figure out if your over-reaction to work stresses might be linked to something else in your life.

There is no easy solution to these problems, no magic wand available or a list of to-dos that can entirely mitigate or solve them. And even though we all hate to admit it, sometimes a person we truly respect may have reached the limit of her ability to provide tough and constructive leadership at that high level and should retreat. The aptitude for managing well in all the seasons and dealing comfortably with all situations of the CEO position is unfortunately not always in everyone who has that responsibility.

PASSION, YES, BUT THE RIGHT KIND

In the business vernacular of the day, the use of the word passion occurs frequently. The clarion call is: You have to have passion if you want to succeed! The assumption: Passion is always good and always delivers the desired positive results. Wrong. In all of these hype statements about passion, very seldom, if ever, do authors differentiate between the different variations of passion. For them, it seems to be one and the same.

In fact, there are two kinds of passion: good and bad. Both exist in very real terms, and one type has—with one exception—absolutely nothing to do with the other type. One type is positively directed and motivating; the other, destructive and demotivating.

Bad passion in a CEO is an exercise in negative extremes: too much fear, doubt, frustration, exasperation, impatience, and too little of the steady, caring consistency necessary for good leadership. Bad passion means no time for niceties, vacation, caring, personal contact, or slight changes of pace to take some of the pressure off and relieve stress. The thought processes of a CEO consumed with bad passion are erratic. He never gets the bad news in a timely fashion because abject fear of retribution hangs in the air, and messengers are reluctant to deliver that news. Bad passion is the birthplace of impatience, hurried decisions, ill-conceived policies and procedures, and "hyperactive attacks" in every direction. The CEO with bad passion criticizes his people in front of others, and uses words that cut deeply into their psyche. Bad passion creates demotivated employees.

Bottom line: Bad passion causes a company and its leadership to be tied up in knots, going nowhere fast.

Contrast that with the benefits and character of good passion. Here you find a CEO who builds on a foundation of experience and expertise, and creates a solid platform for people to strive to reach desirable and transparent goals. Good passion electrifies the organization with energy, drive, and conviction. Good passion comes from a CEO who knows, through solid experience, what she is doing, believes in the direction she is taking the company, and articulates it well. A CEO infused with good passion does not take down her people in front of their colleagues. She strives to spend quality time with the employees of the company, no matter what their station or position may be. She understands their thinking, and if she doesn't, she reaches out to make sure she does.

A CEO who backs up beliefs with behavior that shows integrity has good passion. Good passion enables a CEO to smile, to project focus and steadfastness in her directives, and to fight to make results happen.

Good passion is not able to be learned or taught. Through actions, a person can convey in-depth awareness of good passion and, through words, discuss its positive effects. But, when all is said and done, in most cases, you either have it or you don't have it. Your task is to compare the CEO who practices bad or good passion with your own performance and attitude toward leadership.

COMBATING IT'LL-NEVER-WORK INTIMIDATION: PACKING POWER INTO YOUR CONVICTIONS

One of the major problems facing every manager in his daily work are the doubts that can creep into every decision he makes or is about to make. These doubts can come at you from every direction, both from inside and outside the company. They are the causes of hesitation and indecision, the brakes holding back your momentum. They are the worrisome thoughts you have when you have identified critical success factors; they are the nagging doubts you have when you have spelled out the risks in doing what you intend to do. This is the extra baggage you will always have to carry.

Some of your people will keep their doubts to themselves. Others in your group who are the professional worriers will vocalize their doubts loudly. Still, others will take you aside and want to go through the whole exercise one more time just to make sure that nothing will go awry. You know very well that the decision-making process involves consideration of all possible problems or risks. In your daily work, you can't exactly do a probability analysis or a detailed modeling exercise every time you need to make a decision. But these processes aren't exactly necessary every time there is something to decide, are they?

Now, however, here you are, sitting alone with a new project on your desk, letting all of these doubts and issues go through your head. A major portion of the project is already underway, and when you really think about it, you can almost taste the rewards of its completion. If only it weren't for those other problems staring at you: Doubt intimidation has begun to work its way into your psyche. All kinds of "what-if's" swirl around in your mind, but it would appear you have no other choice than to proceed.

Years ago, there was an executive I knew who was running a major European subsidiary of a leading American toy company. The toy division part of the German company had been losing money for years. He had games and puzzles to sell, but he needed new product. He had just been sent funny-looking, teardrop-form plastic extrusion products with a happy faces on them, and some stubbly hair in different colors coming out of the heads of these "somethings."

The sales director of this company, a man of vast experience, didn't have any doubts about the marketability of this product—he thought it would be an unmitigated disaster. He had determined it would damage the reputation of the company, and expressed his opinion in front of the whole sales force and marketing department.

The CEO had only been in the industry six months and was still learning the subtleties and nuances of the market. At that moment, however, he not only had to stare down the sales director, but also face every other person in the company, because they were all against launching the product. The question for the CEO was this: Was the greater potential damage to be found in launching this product, and possibly not earning money or in not launching and continuing to watch the decline of the company in market importance?

He made a clear decision to launch. The remaining question was how? These were somewhat ugly-looking blobs that needed a creative leg to stand on, including a background story containing elements of the German way of life. The whole group of doubters (basically the whole company) learned that the company was moving ahead. The atmosphere was tense and negative. But the "somethings" had also gone through a transformation: They had now become the Snugglebumms who lived in the forest and sang songs and danced all day. They had fun names and loved life. They were a positive, happy toy for a little girl. The CEO had a solid concept with a direct cultural link. The product went to the market and never even landed on the store shelves. Young girls roared into the toy shops and literally ripped the brown shipping cartons apart to get at the products, most of which hadn't even had price tags put on them yet. The product was an immediate and complete sell-out, and continued to sell strongly for more than a year after that. Sales ran in the multi-millions, and the product was profitable. The CEO stood taller as a result of this. And the sales director was no longer a doubter.

The CEO had been subjected to an enormous amount of doubt intimidation, particularly because his sales director had rarely made a bad call in more than 20 years of working in the industry. What made this CEO go ahead in spite of the doubts?

In this instance, the CEO went out and secured for himself an additional "insurance policy," a good tactic for every CEO to consider when everyone and everything is ganging up on an idea or a decision. He took that "something" that was causing so much bother, inserted it into the fantasy world his marketing people had created, and then personally visited some families who had little girls. He took enough of the product with him to give each of the girls one to play with. He explained what the Snugglebumms did, what they loved, and where they lived. And then he watched. Those little girls didn't stop playing with those toys, so he knew he was on to *something*—potential broad consumer acceptance of the product.

Big doubts among major members of your organization, who rail against a particular decision or concept, *have* to be listened to, and their doubts must be taken seriously. Sometimes a consensus may be very difficult or even impossible to reach. You'll need lots of convincing, lots of talking, and lots of checking of critical assumptions and success factors that could impinge upon that product's success. Your stomach gets into the act as well. In addition, there are always serious financial, market, resource, and production issues to be considered. Yet, every CEO knows that there are times when he must go the lonely road and make an unpopular decision. That is what you get paid for and that is what you are there to do. Prior to making that kind of decision, the smart CEO will sit back, get out of the woods, so to speak, and take a look at the whole forest. And then ask himself the following questions:

- Is there agreement on the need to do the whole project or only on specific points within the project?
- Where and what are the specific doubts and concerns? Are these concerns project-breakers? Are they so serious that the project would have little or no chance of success?
- How do I treat and consider the vocalized doubts and concerns being brought to the table by my colleagues? What arguments would convince them that the project or program is worthwhile to proceed with? Do I sincerely believe in what I am saying? Am I transmitting that belief credibly and effectively?
- What relevance do these concerns have for the overall situation where, without the project, the company might lose momentum or not reach certain goals?
- What, specifically, is it going to take to make this project a success? Do we, as a company, have the talent, drive, and resources to make it happen? What are the critical success factors involved?
- What are the risk factors if the project fails? What will be the costs?

You will need time to think and study all of the alternatives, along with all of their positives and negatives. It is possible that you will decide that the risks are too great, that the doubters, even though they have irritated you, were right in opposing a particular project or program. That solves the problem quite handily. Accept this fact. Compliment your people without rancor on their good thinking, and move on.

Contrarily, assuming that you have really done your homework, that the project return is well above your target ROI, and that you have a possible exit strategy should things go south in the middle of the project, then make the call and prove with conviction and passion that it was the right one. Fact: Once you make such a lonely decision, it is quite amazing to discover that the opposition, which was so adamantly opposed to a particular project, may simply fade away. Instead of continuing to block the move, they will, keying off of your confidence in the project, support it as if nothing had ever been said, and as if there never had been any doubts. These are sometimes quite astounding transformations. Use them to build momentum for what you have decided to do. Help your people feel even better about their new support for the project by working with them on new applications or new market potential, or in designing the hopefully unnecessary fall back positions or exit strategy should the project in question not reach its intended objectives. You don't do the latter because you have doubts, but because this is professional risk management and good business practice, and your people are marching with you now.

NEW CONCEPTS SELDOM FLOW SMOOTHLY DOWNHILL. PRIMEVAL EVENTS ARE PRIMEVAL EVENTS.

Business model changes and shifts in company direction affect nearly every operational part of the company. They can be positive because they make potentially stronger future growth in sales and profits. They can be harmful because the model itself may be based upon false premises or false hopes. They can be dangerous because they can create major problems with your people and their motivation. Never forget that with any change, you are automatically going to those areas where your people will see themselves directly affected by the change: egos, emotions, and protection of turf will be the central factors in this drama. As a consequence, changes in the business model concepts, their preparation, as well as their subsequent execution and its measurement, require detailed and intensive reflection and consideration. Should you worry about this? Mind-set and job content change? The following two examples illustrate these points.

Example 1

You have done your homework. Your board has signed off on a 79-page summary version of your proposed strategic business model change. They have authorized you to begin with the plan's execution and to complete the work within two years. The company has grown rapidly, but it is now clear that a centralized organization can no longer handle the demands associated with operating in a multitude of different markets. It is time to decentralize and create regional units. At the same time, you want to keep the entrepreneurial spirit that has characterized the company and propelled it to its current strong position intact.

You have been with the company for more than 20 years and are now CEO. You are one of the "founding fathers," having grown with the company. You know all of the players in the company. You have analyzed in advance, both centrally and out in the field, how the new structure must be established. Since this is a decentralization strategy, you have paid particular attention to the personnel at headquarters and their possible reactions to a perceived or real loss of power. And you are quite aware of the situation in the regional areas and what newly found breathing room will do for *their* egos.

You know your people have their contacts, networks, and respective turf; they are settled and successful in their positions. Certainly, a lot of change is coming, but you think they are ready for it, and so are you. To make sure the execution functions properly, you have coaches and trainers lined up; the people from your consulting company have produced reams of material, planning pods, and timing frameworks. Your internal transition staff is waiting for the start signal, and the HR department is prepared to meet and master all problems. Nothing wrong with the planning side of the equation.

You have heard the voices of reason: Many of the employees who have been told in the past that they were doing a good job will be consternated by the fact that the company seems to be dramatically changing its business model, and consequently its thinking about the structure and organizational set-up of the company. Everyone knows that this changeover is going to be something of a culture shock, but an even bigger shocker is the fact that there are voices in the hall that maintain that you and your leadership could be the biggest problem of all.

What is going on here? The fact is that you may simply have been in your job too long. Whether you like it or not, you have stood for the merits of a centralized organization for many (maybe too many) years. You have grown up and thrived in it. You are not actually negatively tainted by all of this, but at the same time, you do have a certain history, a certain corporate mentality that is almost part of your business DNA. And when you really are honest with yourself, you know very well that your conflicted attitude about centralization has been influenced by where you came from and how you arrived at where you are.

Perhaps there is an even more serious problem. There are hard personnel decisions to be made involving what positions will be filled and by whom, and who will have to step back or even leave the company. Headquarters will have a number of concerns in this regard. You are going to have a major problem making those hard decisions because you are understandably close to many of the players involved. You hired and trained most of them! As a result, your ability to make the right decisions could be called into question. In short, you may find yourself not only part of the solution, but part of the problem.

If your board hasn't been thinking along these lines because of loyalty to you and the fact that the company is doing well, then they should have been. In fact, they have exactly the same problem you do. They know you and who you are, and what you have not been up to now is a proponent of decentralized organizational thinking and management. You also know deep down that you don't have the experience in doing this sort of thing, so you ask yourself how effective you really can be in bringing the whole program to a successful conclusion.

A suitable answer to this dilemma may lie in your *stepping back*, not stepping down. Does this mean you are opting out of the responsibility? Not a chance. You would simply plan to assign the overall responsibility for the day-to-day operational changeover to a no-nonsense decentralization czar, someone who has already successfully led a major part of the company and has prior experience working in a decentralized company. This czar would be a person of your confidence and would report to you directly. She would be removed from current duties, but certainly have at least a similar, if not even more important, job to return to when the model changes are completed. All authority to effect the change and make the required decisions would be placed in her hands. All major personnel decisions would be handled by the czar and the HR department, whereby you would be involved in the discussions, as well as the final decisions required.

Creating such a position has several additional advantages for you and the company:

- You will be giving the responsibility to someone you hired years ago whose operational acumen you trust and respect.
- You have someone in the position with lengthy experience working in a decentralized company.
- You have someone who knows many of the people who will be affected by the change and who will carefully and fairly consider these people's needs, egos, and turf problems against the background of the overall objectives of the reorganization.
- As CEO, you continue to oversee the whole decentralization endeavor, while at the same time ensuring that the company continues to push toward the overall sales and profits goals set for it.

Example 2

There are times when a new model change can cause major disruption and even direct danger for the company itself. In the case of the following company, a business model change is being planned that will affect, in a very broad and deep fashion, the way the company conducts its business. The change is intended to provide the company with a totally new and different approach to increasing sales in the market.

Go back with me to the early 1980s in Germany, where up-market demand is driving a change in the country's retail scene. Small specialty retail stores, by building core competence in these prime high-margin consumer product areas, are gearing up to take even more of the consumer deutsche mark for themselves. Only two individual department stores have adjusted to the times—one in Berlin and one in Stuttgart. They belong to the competition. Both stores have forged an identity that has them serving every pocketbook. Their emphasis, however, is increasingly on the high end of the non-durable consumer product segment. Their stores are different, they have a different feel. Their sales are correspondingly growing rapidly.

Viewing the situation in the market, and jealous of the success of those two stores, the top management of a leading department store chain sets out on a quest: Management visits other large, successful department stores around the world—United States, Spain, Italy, France, England, Australia, Japan, Hong Kong, Singapore—that seem to be following the same differentiation strategy used by the successful stores in Berlin and Stuttgart. The question they take with them on their odyssey: What are these leading department stores doing that differentiates them in *their* markets? Do their companies have the same problem as our company has in Germany? Top management focuses its visits on what are known in the trade as world-class stores that sell, in addition to their normal goods, up-market and luxury brands in high-class surroundings. What they see, they like. Management's conclusion: exactly the right solution. Why not do the same thing in Germany?

Monies and resources flowed, and analysis upon analysis was done on the company's image and target groups. They considered what they thought to be critical success factors. The board signed off on the investment to remodel and expand the most important stores the company had in Germany. The architects almost danced into the board room with beautiful designs for the interiors. Negotiations commenced with many of the leading brands of the world, some of which balked at going into a department store where they had previously given preference to the very successful specialty retail store trade. Nevertheless, with board approval in hand, and preparations well-advanced, excitement was in the air.

Was it a done deal? Unfortunately not. Not much attention had been paid to what counted the most: the culture, mental fixations, customs, and lifestyle of company personnel, those people who would carry the main responsibility for the success of the concept. Many of the employees came from simpler origins and didn't know or understand the subtlety of brand image and world-class brands, much less selling in an up-market situation. Many of them didn't earn enough to ever consider buying such products.

Instead, management thought their people would be pleased at the company's decision because it meant that company employees would be able to keep their jobs and the chain would continue to survive in an increasingly difficult competitive retail situation. The attitude, never spoken aloud, was more or less the following: *give the employees some training, get them thinking about image, and everything will be just fine.*

This reminds me of George Bernard Shaw's *Pygmalion*, the basis for the musical *My Fair Lady*. Just teach Eliza Doolittle how to say a few words like a Londoner and she'll be a lady.

These people were to be placed "on stage" at the very forefront of the change; they were to be sent into an enormously changed product and market situation and didn't have a clue how that was going to work. They listened to speeches, watched the dancing eyes of managers, and concluded: *This is going to be a problem.* This was not their life, this was not their style, and this was not what they thought they could do.

The stores were slowly remodeled. The plan and its implementation took longer than originally foreseen. Sales lagged behind budgeted revenues. Through time, major shifts in the composition and quality of the personnel occurred. What was the cause of this unexpected, slower realization of the concept? In fact, there was a measure of arrogance in the decision to do what everyone else was doing successfully around the world without adequate, in-depth consideration of the human and cultural side of the equation in their own company. The subtleness of this had escaped management. They had been overwhelmed by a concept that they thought had win-win written all over it.

The lesson in this case is clear: If you are going to introduce major changes in your business model, or the manner in which you approach the market, you must consider the implications for the people of your organization a priority. Assess *in detail* their ability to absorb the model change and make it work. While they may smile with enthusiasm at you when you broach the subject of the planned change, their heads might not be in the same place as yours, and their background, training, and orientation may not mesh with your new demands and standards. They may disagree that such a step is the right one for the company. They will need convincing. They will need to hear about plans and procedures designed *precisely* and *particularly* to address *their* needs, concerns, and must be given time to develop a perspective as to how they see themselves fitting into the new concept. Without their minds *and* their hearts, you could be launching a ship that will never reach a port.

There are times when there are good reasons to treat such sweeping changes on a confidential basis. After all, the current business must go on, and current sales targets must be met. But once you and your top management start to consider the benefits of a possible model change, these are the questions you need to address:

- Is the model simple in design, or so complex that any attempt to execute it, no matter how well intentioned, could possibly result in major, company-endangering difficulties?
- Are the critical underlying assumptions we have used in designing the new model sound?
- Is the additional performance potential we are seeing based on sound economic analysis and estimates of the market and its trends?
- Have all of the key critical success factors that will make the difference between success and failure been identified, considered, and correspondingly fully taken account of?
- Is the manner in which we are "selling" the model change to our people the most appropriate? Will they be able to see the value in the changes for themselves, their jobs, and the company? And do they have the ability to execute the model change effectively? Do we really have their support, or is it only financial realism at work? Have we identified the informal leaders and the most competent individuals inside of the company who will be charged with introducing the model change within the company and at the respective company locations? Are *they* convinced of the merits of the change?
- Have all of the people who will be affected by the model changes been properly trained for any eventual changes in their responsibilities?
- Do we have vacant positions within the organization that could cause us problems in the execution phase? Are we going too fast, and thereby not considering the inherent risk of failing to execute properly because of missing human resources?
- Is our marketing message and image in the public domain so fixed that any change in our model will require large or perhaps excessive capital and promotional expenditures to effect a change in consumer or customer thinking or attitudes about our company? Do we really believe that our marketing plans will elicit a positive response from the market? And how will we, besides using sales volume, correctly measure that response?
- Is the model change going to be credible enough in the market to keep both our current customers buying from us, as well as bring in new customer potential we otherwise would not have seen?

- Has our top management been involved in any training or seminars on change management before introducing the concept/model to the company at large?
- Has management set phased execution targets and review periods after reaching each target to establish potentially new benchmarks, and to take advantage of all factors and problems arising in the preceding phase(s)?
- Are our financial and/or sales targets realistic so that we are not forced, due to below-expectation performance, to delay or even cancel parts of the new model change within the company?
- Finally, do we already have all of the necessary elements in place to make this change a success, or are we depending upon our muddle-through skills to put some of the last and most important parts of puzzle together *after* the execution phase has started?

These questions and well-thought out answers are critical for any successful model change. But even then, business model changes are still the most dangerous and most difficult of management responsibilities. They must be handled with care and due diligence until you are completely satisfied that you have a sound and practicable plan in hand.

In the example of the department store chain, management should have known that luxury up-market brands have more marketplace appeal than just the product and price. The third dimension in luxury selling is image, supported by the advertising message and perception, and qualified personnel. The retail specialty stores, with their owners and long-time sales employees building close personal relationships with their customers, *understood* this fact. The department store management misjudged this critical success factor. Years later, the situation had improved to the point where this department store chain had finally succeeded in building an acceptable up-market retail position with many of the world's leading brands. But the time and the money lost in this particular case stand as stark witnesses to management's failure to adequately appreciate the subtleties of a special market situation and the possible accompanying impact of the change in its prior business model on its own valued employees.

People—what they think and what they are capable of—count for everything.

Key Priorities

- You travel a lot so you occasionally cross borders. What you *don't* want to do is cross the border between toughness and meanness, between thinking about the company and how it can progress, or thinking about yourself and how you can calm the turmoil raging within you. Meanness hurts people—and it will hurt you if you don't find a way back to the toughness side of the equation.

- "Gotta have passion" is the mantra for success in today's business world. Good passion will get you where you want to be. Bad passion will take you down another road, and possibly destroy your company in the process.

- Doubts are healthy reminders that nothing is ever really 100-percent certain. As CEO, in judging your forward plans, you need to respect those little voices of caution, but at the same time, you also need to know exactly how to go about raising those plans' success percentages to the high levels you know are necessary.

- You may have the best of intentions—and plans—to change the way your company conducts its business. But if you haven't thought about the key factor, your people, and how you can mobilize their inherent power and motivation behind that change, then you are heading for a possible debacle.

Chapter 7

Your People— The Soul and Sole Power of the Company

You've heard it over and over again: Leading a company and its employees means knowing you are dealing with likes, dislikes, emotions, egos, thin skins, talent, broad experience, past history, aspirations, separate agendas, as well as the risk of making the wrong choice when you organize your employees for future battle. Every one of these people looks to you for leadership, the right idea, the warning finger, and the calmness in times of stress and severe difficulties. But what will *bond* them together and you to them is the style of leadership you practice. Caring is the magic word. Take a look at the benefits of what *that* kind of leadership will give you.

Hiring and Firing: How to Be On-Target When You Are Off-Location

You have been hired to revamp, revitalize, and redirect the fortunes of a consumer-durable company that has been enduring sales declines and losses for several years. You have done your own personal due diligence on the company, run your detailed SWOT analysis (Strengths, Weaknesses, Opportunities, and Threats), kept your counsel until you have developed a solid and balanced picture of the company, and determined what needs to be done—quickly. A major priority is building an organization with which you can attack and solve those problem areas, both short- and long-term, that have hindered the company from growing and producing an acceptable return for the stakeholders in the past. Time is definitely not on your side. You have the organization chart, but where are the people?

Some of the newly created positions can be easily and immediately filled because there are excellent people already on board who are fully qualified for several of the new positions. They are your automatic "keepers." You should also consider those who allegedly didn't do so well under the previous administration. Your predecessor has told you that "these people" would likely be the ones you would need to replace. But you have seen and heard this kind of thing before, and are well aware that there could have been a difference of opinion or a leadership issue between the CEO and his top people in the past that could have caused this kind of comment. So you scrutinize everybody and make up your *own* mind about them. You discern there are several who have shown that they *are* capable individuals, effective and brimming with good ideas. It often happens that an executive under one type of leadership and in one specific type of company situation will unfortunately perform below his capabilities and thereby suffer image problems and criticism of his performance. But get him into a different setting under new leadership, and that performance dynamic can readily change. Whatever the reason may be, and some of it could be due to the "new beginning" in the company, or perhaps your more open leadership style, you have unlocked some previously underestimated management talent. That will certainly help in filling the positions on your organization chart, saving you money and time in the process.

You have also scoured the company looking for talented individuals with potential who could be entrusted with one or several of the key positions you need to fill. You have found several interesting people you feel could potentially do the job. If you are honest with yourself, though, you know that you and the company need people who can hit the ground running. Unfortunately, while perhaps interesting and viable candidates for future advancement, the internal candidates you have identified at the secondary or tertiary levels within the organization may not be appropriate solutions for your immediate needs. Nevertheless, maybe there is one in the group who you decide to put on the chart. She is being fast-tracked and knows it, but you have confidence in her that she can grow quickly into the job.

As a stopgap, you do have an assistant or two within the respective divisions who can take up some of the work on a temporary basis, and you can have one or two of the other executives take on some extra duties. Furthermore, some of the work could be done by you personally, on a limited basis. But these are interim measures and temporary fixes, and not the modus operandi designed to enable you to do what you need to do: turn around the company and get it moving again.

However, as you look at your organization chart, you know you are still facing a major task. Three very key executive positions remain unfilled. As you proceed, remember that moving too fast when it comes to hiring can hurt rather than help. This immediate need could turn into a classic no-win situation for you. If you hurry the search, turning to an executive search firm, you will get some candidates. They are often people who the recruiter already knows and finds competent. Everything on paper will most likely fit the profile you have established. But you know because so many things are pressing that you personally can only spend a limited amount of time interviewing each candidate. Perhaps you will be able to break loose some time to go to dinner with him and his spouse or companion in order to get to know him better. That still may not be enough time interacting, with enough diversity in the interaction to get a well-rounded picture of the person. But you must act and you must decide.

If you are in a hurry, you may find yourself rationalizing or excusing comments that you have heard from several of the final fast-track candidates and minimizing character traits that don't appeal to you, thereby leaving you vulnerable and pursuing a path of risk. It is possible that you might get lucky with your choice, but more likely not. On the other hand, instead of the hurried approach, you might decide that you are going to take the time necessary to find the right people, regardless of the immediate need. When you are still looking six months later, you realize that going slower could be as much a mistake as hurrying. This is a dilemma, no matter how you look at it.

Disentangle yourself from the underbrush and consider what the whole forest looks like. The reality is that by hurrying, you are running the risk of choosing the wrong person in the heat of the moment and losing more than a whole year of effectiveness in the position you are trying to fill. Take a look at what can happen:

- **The first three months:** The new hire gets acquainted with the position and the responsibilities, while supposedly gaining some solid footing in the company.
- **The second period of three to five months:** You suspect or have already determined that the person who was hired for the job isn't going to cut it.
- **The third period of three to four months:** A new search is initiated, with the person either still in the job, because you need somebody doing something in there, or already out of the company, because the whole situation had become unbearable and detrimental to the company's interests.
- **The déjà vu period:** You are back again to the first three-month period, albeit this time with an intensely higher sense of urgency. And one year has gone by.

This flameout is pain. You will feel the punishment of having rationalized a candidate's strengths and minimized weaknesses, ignored your intuitive distaste for what the person said, and depended upon the executive recruiter to do all of the reference work instead of personally conducting any due diligence. Your time investment may have been a maximum of eight to 10 hours of meetings with each one of the candidates. Psychological assessment, as well as a thorough check of references, also took place, as prescribed for such positions. But what has really happened? On one hand, you have spent some important on-site time with each of the candidates. On the other hand, this one-sided approach to location can be a very superficial one and, at times, even dangerous when one considers the enormous risk of losing a whole year's time because the wrong candidate was chosen for the job.

To get a more in-depth reading on the candidate, consider how meeting in a different location and environment could give you a different perspective on the opportunities and risks related to an individual. You should meet your candidate in a *variety of situations* because she may very well adapt her persona to each of those situations, showing sides of herself you never experienced or suspected before. She has, of course, a clear opportunity to convince you again of her aptitude and qualifications for the position, or, finding herself in a non-business environment, she may risk saying or doing things she wouldn't normally do in your office or at your home. You may very well find one or more of these persona adaptations to be inappropriate for the position in question. Conversely, you may be able to confirm your positive opinion of your candidate.

While hiring a Director of Sales, I met three or four times with the same candidate, but always in the office or at a meeting, or in a formal lunch situation off campus. Everybody in the company was positive about this person, including myself, but I couldn't escape the feeling that I wasn't seeing and hearing who this person really was. And so, for two Saturdays in a row, I went for a long walk in the woods with him, stopping at different locations along the way for some refreshments. During one stop, he started talking about things we had never discussed before. He made comments on his surroundings and his frustrations about life—even derogatory remarks about the people at the next table. After the stop, he continued to make disparaging remarks about people passing by us. And there they were: the prejudices, the negativity, the arrogance—reasons not to hire him.

In another situation, I was sitting with a candidate in an outdoor cafe next to a table where a mother was holding her baby son. I had the pleasure of listening to this person tell me how, at a turning point in his life, he had been motivated, in part, to choose business as a career because of the influence of his mother. Earlier, in the more formal interview setting, he had responded very well to the question of what had motivated him to choose his particular discipline. Satisfactory, straight forward, and business-like, but not moving— nor the real reason, as it turned out. But as he spoke in the cafe that day, I saw tears in his eyes; he spoke of his mother putting her hand on his arm and he spoke thankfully of her encouraging him to continue with his studies after he had gone through an unhappy divorce during his university years. From there, he moved the discussion to how important it was for him to care about people and to take time to work with them and motivate them. Showing feelings, and perhaps weakness, was not unacceptable. It was compelling. I knew his job experience, and now I knew the person. I hired him minutes later. And in the following years, he put together some of the finest "sales music" I have had the pleasure of experiencing.

Personas change. People let down their guard. People think that by making hard or negative comments (which they really believe), they will be able to create a positive impression among the people listening to them. They think they are showing how tough they can be. How very wrong, and how destructive for advancing one's career.

Your executive recruitment decision-making is more complex if you are looking at the same time for multiple candidates for key positions. In spite of the additional time and coordination efforts involved, it is advisable to engage several executive recruiting firms, each of whom would look for one candidate for one of the various positions. These firms will know that there are other colleagues of theirs in the game; they will see where you are guiding the organization and see future business potential for themselves, so they will work extra hard to make sure that you get what you are looking for. This healthy competition serves your purpose, and you will most likely get the optimum performance possible from each of these firms.

And what if you find yourself at the other end of the spectrum? Someone is not performing, and there is dissatisfaction in the ranks. In practically every case, unless there are extenuating circumstances of perhaps a private nature, there will be a lot of thrashing around and holding of the head in desperation when mistakes are made by the person in question, unsatisfactory attempts are made to give the person a chance in spite of everything, and working with the person to perhaps improve the situation. Unfortunately, this rarely works.

As difficult as it is, there is only one solution that is not only fair to the company, but also to the person involved because she will know how close the cut is and will be going through her own personal hell because of it. Close the chapter. Quietly and fairly let the person go without delay. If you haven't done it already, initiate your search for a new person as quickly as possible.

When it comes to hiring, invest your time, and check the personas of your candidate. If you take your time with firing, you waste time.

CHARACTER AND GENES: PRIMING YOUR SUCCESSION PIPELINE WITH THE RIGHT PEOPLE

The work of building a staff isn't all done when new people, whatever their position in the company, come on board. The need for schooling and/or training in the respective disciplines never goes away. Neither does reinforcing the way your people in the company approach put those disciplines successfully to work.

Training, improving performance, motivating, raising the knowledge bar, increasing effectiveness, building depth, being up-to-date, and widening horizons are all issues integral to management's to-do training list, and their justification to do something on a continual basis to raise the quality of job performance. It is simply good business.

But be careful here. We are talking major and possibly continued expense. The training may also be aimed at more than the mechanics of the job. Training can also take aim at redirecting or reorienting individual human character and conduct.

- Company personnel must be trained in the basics of their jobs, in product knowledge, or in the policies of the company as these policies relate to internal performance standards and to serving the customer.

- Investments made in these areas on a continued basis with competent trainers and supervisors are absolutely necessary, and should be given high priority. There are training people in the industry who are not charlatans and who offer real substance and results. A CEO who ignores giving his people sound operations training, who doesn't allocate investment money on a continued basis for these activities, is laying the groundwork for serious problems, both in the short and long terms.

But what about the people themselves—their characters, personalities, actions and reactions, emotions, stress tolerance, basic attitude toward their fellow man, and their ability to express themselves and to convince and sell concepts or products?

Training institutes and trainers are a multi-billion dollar industry. Any number of trainers with resumes the length of two of your arms will visit and tell you, "Mr. CEO, I can take your people and make them change the way they think and act. And all of this, of course, to the benefit of your company and its competitive position." And then they go for the close: "I can take competent, even the somewhat hesitant and introverted employees, and turn them into_____." Fill in the blank: motivating and positive model leaders, salesmen, plant supervisors, service representatives. What the CEO listening to this pitch is experiencing is quite easy to imagine: the end of the rainbow. However, this is the same CEO who worries about the operational time factor, who is concerned that there are not enough hours in the day for his people to do their jobs. So in his mind, he starts a game of tradeoffs: *This is important, but it costs a lot of money, but this guy is a pro, and my people do expect it and they will profit from it (I hope).*

There is another side to this equation that seldom, if ever, gets put on the scales when such a formal training contract is considered, that is, the quality of your people measured in terms of their basic, natural ability to absorb and practice the "new way." Can they carry forward that which they have learned about themselves and their interaction with their colleagues or customers, and use it effectively and routinely in every appropriate operational situation?

Most people do come out of such training experiences motivated at a very high level, even those for whom such seminars represented some form of stress and perhaps showcased their "inadequacies." Later, most of these people will remember something they have learned or practiced, and try it out in a real-life setting. But when the daily stress sets in again, when there are 60 minutes in the hour and they need 120 to do everything, the natural tendency for most of the people will be to revert back to who they were before the training, before they received their certificate of completion. And then they stay there. The return on investment was a short-lived gain.

Before you begin or change your training program, approach the problem in the following manner: Consider that there are really only two major groups of people involved in such training in any company: the 45 percent people and the 85 percent people. The first category are the hard-working people who are perfectly competent in their jobs, and without whom the company could not operate. They suffer mightily when asked to make radical changes in their work and their behavior, such as speaking extemporaneously, or striding with conviction from their seats to the front of the room to address the group.

The 85 percent people have the personality and ability to absorb new ideas, to mold and fold them into their already very effective way of operating or conducting themselves, and to do so in a way that makes them appear as if they had been using those ideas all of their lives. They are the ones who will really benefit from the training seminars. These are the employees with potential to be driving forces in your company, and who are candidates for higher positions. You are looking at your *succession pipeline*, so making a major investment in such training for them is more than worthwhile.

I once observed the CEO of a major multinational consulting firm wrestle with the question of training for his lead consultants and managers. Essentially, he wanted to improve their selling, consulting, and negotiating techniques through a series of training sessions aimed primarily at adjusting their personalities so they would be more effective for the company in the market. Consultants are generally not in their profession because they missed out on being selected as lead salesmen, negotiators, or motivational spirits. They are there because they have, among other things, an extraordinary feeling for numerical, operational, strategic, or abstract issues. Some of them are good in client and interpersonal relations; some are not.

Yet, here was the CEO thinking of a broad-based "personality, social and emotional competence, and character training" investment aiming the *same* content at all of the people in his company. The well-meaning advice given him as he tried to make his decision was the following: identify and select only the 85-percent people according to specific profiles and selection benchmarks, and let the 45-percent people continue to do what they do well. Give them the training they must have in their respective disciplines, but let it go after that. In spite of this advice, the CEO, convinced that he had the makings of a major qualitative improvement close at hand, made a major investment in all of his people, involving not only costs for the training seminars themselves, but also lost opportunity costs to the company in the form of non-billable time.

What results were achieved? Respectively, quite a bit, and almost none. The 85-percenters learned some good new tricks and methods, and could incorporate them in their future work. They have been "improved" by the training, and reinforced/motivated by knowing that they had performed well in the training. Contrasting that, the 45-percenters displayed practically no effect. They were happy to get out of the training when it was done.

The lesson for the CEO here is clear: If you think that behavioral change can be achieved, then make the investment. In doing so, however, make sure that the composition of the audience is carefully considered, and that fair and balanced personnel profiles are established for use in the selection process. One size does not fit all.

In addition, make sure that the training program you choose does not languish. One-off training seminars are generally a waste of time, money, and effort. With most people, for such a program to be really effective and reinforcing, particularly for your 85-percent people, the right trainer with the right credentials must be engaged, and the training must have continuity to it, as well as your continued and direct support.

As far as measuring this kind of investment in terms of effectiveness, you are going to be confronted with forms and follow-up interviews in order to qualitatively check how your people are applying what they have learned. The real primary effect, however, is going to be motivational—and perhaps subtle—for the right people, because you are dealing with your best and most receptive employees. Your concerns about finding succession candidates for your top people will definitely be reduced because of it.

How can one then put all that into something that is quantitatively or qualitatively sound? How does one measure improved confidence in a meeting or stronger attitude when the going gets tough? You can't. The chances are much greater that you'll be netting something from your efforts if you make sure from the very beginning that your team is mostly composed of 85 percenters.

As CEO, you should be the first to recognize the truth in all of this. After all, are you really going to sit there with a straight face and deny that you aren't among the strongest and the fittest of them all?

OFFICE POLITICS: IS TOLERANCE EVEN AN ALTERNATIVE?

This office is ground zero.

All one can hear in the company is a low-grade buzz, and it's not coming from your customers trading positive comments on the merits of your new product line. And why are there closed office doors where there should be none? Why are some of the known company "mobbing gangs" going to lunch together (invite yourself to lunch with them one of those times and have some fun) or meeting outside the company for a quick drink? Who or what is going on, and how is that going to take place?

Conniving and scheming individuals are good at hiding the dirt and, at the same time, arrogant in thinking that no one is picking up on the signals. You are, though, because you have positioned your reliable "listening posts" from whom you are receiving messages. You recognize the intermittent bad buzz. You are dealing with degrees of intensity, not a true stop and start. You know how distracting and enervating all of this can be and how it can take a company off of its game and effectively away from the direction in which it should be heading.

If you yourself are part of the problem, that is, if you play right up there in the front row with everybody else, then you might want to consider whether your title is CEO, or high-level corporate rumormonger. If that is not the case, then you should consider taking the following steps to mitigate or eliminate the more blatant and harmful effects of office games and the rule of the mob.

The warning shot.

One of the most important things you can do is recognize that much of office politics revolves around your people thinking that, through their agitating, they can directly impact and influence what is going to happen. It may be a personnel situation, a change in the organization, the strategy of the company, or whatever their agenda includes. They aim to get the masses going because they think they have a chance to force a change. You have to be straightforward. First, don't participate in any of these politics, and second, make explicitly and publicly clear that political machinations or games are never going to be the deciding factor in any tactical or strategic decision made by you or the company. You can add some additional "warning shot" effects to that message. You will know the player or players, those who are at the center of any games going on. During a normal business discussion on an entirely different subject with one of the persons involved, you can bring your displeasure and opinion on the events of the day into the discussion. If you do this in a hidden way, so that the person involved thinks you don't know what he is doing or what is going on, then you can really push the subject hard and attack the problem. Don't worry. The message will be very clearly understood. He and his fellow travelers know you are not stupid, and they think they aren't either. Don't count on this working or stopping the games every time, but it is a useful initial tactic you can use to try to combat the problem.

Upping the ante.

Ask yourself if the offense wouldn't be the more effective means than defense as a way to defuse the situation. You may have already concluded, for example, that part of the problem may lie in the fact that a wall has grown between you, your managers, and the people in the company. It's that vague yet pervasive feeling that the company is not working as one whole, but rather in several parts. People are saying what they feel: Nobody knows what is happening in this company; there are many rumors with nothing being done to blunt the politics and remove the oxygen that feeds the fires. The prescription for this kind of situation can be expressed in one short phrase: *information bursts.* These would be contained within your office's normal communication and information output. This does not mean you refer in any way directly to the rumors in these communications. Be more subtle, and use this technique *within* all of the other general subjects you address to talk directly and boldly to those particular themes of the day. This draws a line in the sand, and says, "I *know* what you people are about, and this is where *I* stand."

End game time.

Be prepared to take firmer steps than the previous two, should the "co-operative" or "informative" touch not eliminate most of the problem. Office politics will never go away; where there are people, there are office politics. And where there are office politics, there are usually several supposed leaders, namely people who seem to spend a lot of time doing nothing but influencing and manipulating the people around them. Don't think that you can transfer these people out of such situations and thereby remove their support system. They will just build a new one in the department where they have been transferred. Consequently, there may be no other alternative but to take them out of the job and out of the company. In preparing this step, you will want to involve your HR department. They will work with you to bring together a multiple and complete record of transgressions and warnings in the file to ensure that the company is protected, and that you have a sound and legal basis to take the steps you will be taking.

Do not prolong the agony. These people are harming your plans, risking the security of other people's jobs, and negatively impacting the company through diverting time and resources to personal agenda games. Don't worry about the public perception of taking this action. This is precisely what you want: immediate knowledge in the public domain of the decision(s) you have made.

Consider the unthinkable and a new approach.

You just may want to sit down and do some serious thinking about your own leadership style and the kind of motivation you currently give to your employees. Office politics will never go away, but there are several basic things you should consider doing, depending upon your character and your own personal style, to keep most of the negative effects of politics and its repetitive character out of the daily life of your company. One of the most important measures is considering the middle- and long-term advantages of being a caring and accessible leader.

Caring Is Part of Your Job Description

After all of the problems you face with personnel agendas and office politics, you might think there really is no sense at all in doing what you do because the dark side is always getting in the way. But you have it in your hand to create something that, without a doubt, can be *the* driving force behind a positive emotional culture in your company and superior results in your marketplace. With your mindset and skills, you can drastically minimize the agenda and office politics games that can or threaten to dominate your company landscape. You are the key to a happy and contented hum in the air.

During the time you have been in the company, you have given of yourself to your people, reached out to them, said "thank you" to them, and have recognized their value as human beings and as employees of the company. You have communicated often and openly with them and, in return, your employees have a sense of ease to do the same with you. You have treated them as equals, taken them seriously, recognized their contributions, and verbalized your appreciation both one-on-one and in meetings. There is nothing that shows caring more than showing your people that you are grateful for their work by noticing it and honoring it with a heartfelt "thank you." ·

If you have done those things, your people will intensely admire you. They will feel valued, connected, and respected. You will have touched the nerve that makes the difference between business by the numbers and business because my CEO cares. You will engender those all-important "I also care" feelings in them. They will want to be near you, and follow you wherever you want to take them. The sub-agendas will fade into the background, and the office politics will be reduced to an almost inconsequential factor in your company's daily life.

However, if you generally don't like people and don't have empathy for them, then you have a problem. Even if your forte happens to be finance, production, economics, or law—areas where supposedly a caring personality wouldn't normally be an overly important factor in leadership—it still doesn't make any difference. There is *no excuse* for not caring. If you don't understand that those who have made mistakes can rise again when you give them support and a helping hand, if you consider your people to be machines who can be slotted into different job categories where their performance will be judged without empathy or understanding, if you are approachable only through appointment, if you actually like the thrust and parry of office politics, then you are a CEO who is not connected to your people, or their real interests, concerns and needs. Don't doubt it for a moment. There is a high price to be paid for "leading" in this fashion.

Your leadership cannot be duplicitous. Never doubt it. Your people see and hear more than you will ever imagine. And they know exactly what you are doing or not doing. If they hear you talking about the corporate family and how "important" that is, if they hear you spouting sweet nothings about employees being the central point of the company, while, at the same time, watching you and seeing that disconnect, many of them—some of them consciously, some of them unconsciously—could very well be looking around for the exit. And if they are not doing so, they probably should be.

Your leadership cannot be mechanical. You can spend hours consulting with every top drawer guy from every training or motivational company who will approach you, doing all of the "right" things to motivate your people, and still get nowhere. Those gestures are just cold, shallow statements if you do them as part of a formula for success, and not as a genuine commitment to your employees' growth.

You maintain that you see the importance of touching the "soul" of your employees, and the core of their identity and happiness. But if you personally are not directly and visibly involved in practicing this policy, then you will have totally missed the central point. *You* are that point. *You* are the third dimension. It is you who must provide the *conviction* to make this kind of motivation credible instead of your efforts being viewed as just something you are doing by the numbers, or because good companies, "do these things."

Many years ago, I did not realize the full value of caring—and showing it. As CEO, I had just taken over a complex and troubled company that needed to be shown the way forward, and I was struggling at the beginning to find it. During that time, a person whom I hardly knew, as I was relatively new in the company, informed me that he had been diagnosed with a serious form of cancer. In spite of this, his doctors were not reacting to his concerns and worries as he wished. He was being forced to wait for additional appointments, and during that waiting time, was going through the hell of uncertainty.

I became disturbed and finally angry in reaction to his plight. I got involved immediately, and spent considerable time during the coming months getting this man his doctor's appointments, a quiet room and bed, and a personal nurse in the clinic for the more complicated tests, while personally reassuring his wife of the company's concern for her husband and our intentions to help him—and her—to the best of our abilities.

During this time, I repeatedly interceded with the hospital, the doctors involved, and the insurance company to help someone who could not really fight for himself because he was a gentleman and perhaps just a little too polite to push hard for what he really needed. My motivation during all of this was very simple: He needed help, and I was in a position as CEO to give it to him.

Time passed, and it came as it had to come. He died and was buried quietly in the late summer of that year. A great sadness came over me, and I expressed this sadness in a speech to a gathering of managers and supervisors in the company. I spoke to them about him and what it had meant to him to have his life somewhat extended, and what it meant to me in taking away some of the worries and concerns he and his family had. I had in no way done all of this with any ulterior motive in mind, but simply because I cared for him as a human being—and as a member of my team and our company. Everyone felt I would have done, under the same circumstances, the very same thing for them.

People in the company were equally sad that day. But then, in the days afterward, I noticed that a tremendous bonding had in fact taken place between them and me. The whole company atmosphere had changed. Their looks, their attitudes, and their body language told me that I had touched them in an extraordinary manner: I had touched their souls. They knew who I really was, that I cared, and what I cared about. Soon after that, we found the right strategy to restart the sales and profit machine of the company. And the sales and profits soared and soared. Yes, in the business sense, the strategy and its execution counted, but the fuel behind all of this was the positive morale and atmosphere in the company. Everybody was going in the same direction, and we all knew why.

Perhaps important to my longer-term development and attitude toward people, I had experienced something that means more than anything else in the successful management of a company: the importance and presence of a leader at the top who really cares and who shows it, unselfishly, unabashedly, consistently, and without ulterior motive. After many years, I left this company for another position with another company, but still today, the core group of managers and employees of this company, including myself, meet once a year for dinner to reminisce about those days long past and how we—all of us—did something extraordinary. And we never forget to talk about why.

There should be no mistake in interpretation or in the message here: As CEO, you are running a business, and responsible for increasing the value of that business for the stakeholders. That is not the point of discussion at hand. Nor is this subject about something that some might call "softness," because some might believe that emotions and sensitivities could perhaps get in the way of the CEO running the business the way he should. But the performance of your people cannot be optimal if the group mentality is, "Why go the extra mile for someone who doesn't even go the standard mile?" If you are that type of CEO, you can rest assured that your people are very likely disconnected from you, and dislike you in a way you wouldn't like and wouldn't even understand.

Your people may not be obvious in their pushback, because they have financial needs relative to their families or to themselves. A good example of this is found in one of our large corporations in the United States. Tens of thousands of employees will not push back against a non-caring and cold CEO who, without a caring word, but professing to have an interest in steadying the company, has repeatedly reduced their overall income and benefits while at the same time earning millions for himself. They won't push back because they need their jobs and the income to care for their families. They are angry and rebellious and feel—and that is the worst part of it—devalued.

But if the CEO (and the board, which is just as guilty) were to question the employees, and obtain an honest answer to their question about the company's leadership and the state of the caring factor within this company, the company would benefit from the honest interchange and be put into an entirely different state of mind. Its customers and its bottom line would surely benefit. Unfortunately, the unhappy consequences of turning away from this reality are missed opportunities in every direction and a continuation of employee devaluation under an insensitive "leadership."

It is astounding how badly some CEOs or owners blunder in such situations and, in doing so, manage to insult their employees in the crassest manner. Their anger or frustration with a particular set of circumstances supersedes their ability to temper those emotions by reining in their tendency to strike out and insult the very people upon which the company depends for its success.

So what are some of the things a CEO can do to "interface successfully?" Here are some of the policies and procedures you should consider as your guide:

- **Be credible.** The first thing you *don't* want to do is to talk constantly about how much you care for your employees and their lives, careers, and health. Talking about all of the benefits the employees have doesn't really help, either. The more you talk about it, without any backup or proof that what you say is actually being lived in the company, and by you, the less credible you are. Never forget that the company has glass walls. Aside from everything else they know about, everyone knows what *you* are doing and thinking, and what you believe in or don't believe in. It is astounding how people can differentiate between hollowness and firmly held beliefs.

- **Stay current on the benefits factor.** Check to make sure that all of the policies established for the benefit of the employees are up to date, that they are somewhat more generous than industry standard (if financially possible), and that they are being applied uniformly and fairly throughout the whole company. You should have your HR department give you and your top executives a monthly or bi-monthly report on benchmarks you will have established to give everyone a clear, in-depth, and broad picture of the employee situation, and the programs affecting employees' well-being. To avoid this report appearing in a somewhat sanitized fashion, you should, when you are sick or have a claim, go through the exact same process in submitting those claims as any of your people do. You will see a functioning system, one where there are errors, or one where the benefits are perhaps inadequate. If the scenario is the latter, then your attention is needed to address the situation. You may also occasionally experience a particular case where you personally have been informed about an employee's situation and medical issues. This is a good check-up opportunity for you. In such cases, carefully and continuously follow the insurance company's performance, as well as that of your own HR department in order to make sure that the caring factor is being uniformly and effectively applied by those carrying the primary responsibility for its resolution.

- **Multiply the caring effect.** Your executives and managers should understand your priority in making supportive leadership one of the most important core values in the company. Being accessible, engaging in proactive listening to employees, and helping employees over rough spots or difficult problems in the company (or even the private ones) are part of this mindset and spirit. This policy and its daily application are particularly important when considering what executive to put in place as the responsible HR Manager. Put the caring factor at the top of the list during the selection process and in all performance reviews.

- **Stay as private as you can.** If you lead a more opulent lifestyle, there is nothing wrong with that. There is also no problem with someone writing an article about you and your family once in a while. However, don't show off your lifestyle, don't talk about it, don't get it out there for everyone to see just because you are involved in "my boat, my car, my house" warfare with other executives, and it is important that this month you pass out the comeuppance award. You can't do this and talk credibly at the same time about the little people and their financial or medical pain, and what the company is doing about it. If you want to be taken seriously, minimize any tendencies of braggadocio, stay with the caring side of the equation, and live your life as you please, but don't make a public affair of it.

- **Get out of your office.** Do a lot of management by visiting around. This will give you the opportunity to meet and talk with many of the people who carry a major part of the load in your company. Take the time to chat with them. And to listen to what they are saying and what they are *really* saying. Comment on any pictures they may have on their desk. Tease them a little about not working too much, and shake their hands and say thank you for their efforts on the company's behalf.

- **Give credit where credit is due.** In any of your official speeches about the company, make a conscious effort to include specific people and their contribution in your remarks. It is nice to hear about creating new jobs, the economy, and the percentage growth of the company sales last quarter, but get it down to the credible and human level. Everybody knows the "top line strut;" they have heard it a thousand times. But imagine the motivational effect that citing the names of your employees in speeches or press releases will have not only on those employees, but also on the attitude of the people around them who see that outstanding performance. By giving credit where credit is due, you are demonstrating unequivocally that you are aware of and thinking about your people deep into the organization, what they are doing, how they are working, and what contribution they are making to the company as a whole. Caring means making time and going the extra mile to demonstrate to your people that everybody is important, and everybody counts.

- **Work with your HR department.** It is important that your HR department keeps you abreast of any serious personnel situations, be they medical or otherwise, where the company could possibly help. Have a box of cards that you can use to write a short note to the person or people involved. In addition, have your HR department and management keep you aware of any awards your people may have received, or any recognition they have experienced for a special contribution within their department or division, and write them a small congratulatory note as well. Be specific about the subject in your congratulations. Be sure to spell the person's name correctly. Then sign the note in good old-fashioned ink.

In all of this, there must be *visible genuineness* in the way you approach these steps. You must be committed to recognizing and respecting the human factor in your company. And the reward? The pleasure of leading a company in which employees grow their skills and knowledge in a supportive atmosphere and then perform in a manner one would not have thought possible. But the greatest pleasure of all is clearly the opportunity for a CEO to stand in the middle of a group of his employees and to sense the specialness of belonging, the positive feeling of the moment, and, above all, the effects of his caring leadership.

Key Priorities

- Personas adapt to surroundings. Candidates for a top position in your organization will often make a good impression under one set of circumstances, such as your office, and maybe a dinner. Take them elsewhere and spend time with them. If they are going to disappoint you, they will do it then. It is better to learn this beforehand.

- Training is good. It's better to make the correct and appropriate choice of which of your people receives what specific training. Your succession policy depends partially upon selecting the 85-percenters for training, those who can absorb not only job knowledge, but also impulses that can contribute further to improving their already positive personality and character attributes.

- Office politics represent a major challenge to the leadership of your company. Your policy must be one of no-tolerance. To effect that, you need to engage in sending some subtle, but also very clear, signals about the consequences. Your people need to know there is no alternative. Every one of the consequences is not pleasant.

- Caring isn't just a word. It is an attitude, an approach, a hope, a concern, the ability to put yourself in the position of another person and understand what will "move" him. If you care and show it, your people will reward you. If you don't, you won't even see him go the standard mile, much less the extra one.

Chapter 8

ASSUMPTIONS— JUST THAT AND NOT MUCH MORE

Your charge is not to lead your company into the past, but into the future. That involves putting a numerical framework around that which you and your people think the company can achieve going forward. Unfortunately, nobody really knows exactly what that future will bring. That fact leaves your company with only one set of tools to use when putting together budgets: historical performance, macroeconomic assumptions, critical success factors and assumptions impacting your ability to make the budget "happen", and a whole series of hopefully good estimates. Call it a best-guess exercise. Take the following sections and their contents to heart: Correctly considered and applied, the lessons contained therein should take away many of the rough edges surrounding those best guesses.

FORECASTING: THE SEMI-ACCURATE GUESSING GAME

You can't run away from the responsibility to be directly involved in forecasting. Forecast continuously, and you could create the disaster of all disasters for the company—and yourself. You need forecasts for just about everything that affects the operational integrity of your company: purchasing, unit sales, inventory level, sales territory, profit, sales volume, margin by product, product performance, shipping and arrival, inflation rate, currency exchange rate, interest rate, operation cost, new product manufacturing cost, and so on. Initially, all of these forecasts will flow into and become part of an official budget. Several months after the new budget year is underway, that budget will go through a transformation and appear under a different name: latest forecast, current projections, or whatever the company chooses to call its latest analysis of the running business year. Clearly, the original budget remains the *valid* budget against which everything will still be measured, but the latest forecast contains the more current, and hopefully more accurate, view.

Every one of these forecasts, if done badly or inaccurately, has the potential to cause both disruptive and costly disasters for the company. Some forecasting people who think they know what they are doing will say to do it from the top down; some will say to do it from the bottom up. Some will do both and see if the numbers meet somwhere; some will say do it by customer; some will say to do by channel of distribution. Sound like a game? It isn't. This is very serious stuff.

Educated guessing is sometimes the name given for the practice of forecasting. Educated guessing implies risk that you could possibly look in the wrong direction. The problem is that every part of this exercise revolves around only one thing: the future. For that reason, you are not going to nail it every time. In fact, it is possible you may never nail it at all. In most cases, bad guesses, combined with unexpected events, will lead only to mild consequences for your company. Unfortunately, the toxic brew resulting from the combination of these two factors can also have severe consequences, or even very severe (very expensive) consequences. Whether mild or severe, the red thread running through all of your forecasting is called "best guess."

Occasionally, you and your people are going to blow by the right numbers and land right in the middle of the wrong ones.

There are multiple factors and data that can help serve as a basis for your forecasting work—modeling, extrapolation, forecasting groups, focus groups, telephone marketing, seasonality weighting, history, tabulating questionnaire responses, calls to economic forecasting shops, sales team forecasts, purchasing benchmarks, Top 25 customer order history, minimum reorder quantities, adjustable blanket orders with minimums, market share assumptions, critical success factors from the past, critical model assumptions, advertising/media reach and effect, channel of distribution inventories (current), purchasing manager attitudes, technical testing under supposed user conditions, past promotional history with spending variables and effects, number of participating customers, customer financial condition and open-to-buy. Regardless of how you do it, in the end, achieving a realistic forecast depends also on what you and your people do with such information. And, more often than not, what you do involves judgment calls.

Expect certain uncomfortable operational events to rev up your stress level. They might include a bad fourth quarter surprise on profits; missing parts and components to produce the forecasted volume of product to be pipelined during your latest new product launch; currency exchange costs (unfortunately hedged only partially due to management uncertainty and option contract costs); lower-than-expected new product sales and margins; large blanket purchasing orders arriving concurrently with the product or product group starting to die an unexpected death in the marketplace, or your continuing to use your largest customer's projected purchases in your forecasted sales revenue numbers while, at the same time, negotiating with him not to stop buying from your company because of his continuing anger at your company's quality control abilities.

Consider this example. In April, although originally built into the budget, you had to indefinitely postpone a price increase of 4.6 percent across your entire product range (sales and margin improvements were included in the forecast/budget) due to unforeseen market contingencies. On an annual budget year basis, you are now missing approximately 3.4 percent of your planned sales dollar volume and, even worse, you're missing the resulting margin increase you had told the board about, as well as the correspondingly higher overall profit forecasts. What else are you missing? To put it bluntly, you are missing an accurate forecast to guide you and your management in moving the company ahead.

If you are CEO of a larger corporation, then you will probably have a central forecasting group within your organization. Your CFO will most likely also be part of this group. In its daily work, the group will continually consult with the operations people in your divisions and subsidiaries regarding relevant information needed for preparing preliminary or final budgets. In addition, they will be drawing upon other resources, such as banking partners, consultants, economist panel members, or other relevant groups whose generated data might be useful for the forecasting process. These people and their output are critical parts of your operational equation. They are not the "nerds" or just the "staff officers" of the organization; these people impact just about everything the company does or doesn't do, and the last time I looked, that is the equivalent of a lot of power. It's power for the good if they hit their numbers, but power for the bad if they miss. In any case, these people should have direct access to the other central power in the organization—you.

If you happen to be in a good mood on a particular day, reexamine the budget black book from previous years, and ask yourself how many faulty guesses/forecasts were contained in it. You can't even begin to count them. Take an additional look at the percentage of correct forecasts made in relation to the total of all of your forecasted numbers for the last year. Your conclusion from all of this can only be as follows: *I know well enough that forecasts contain assumptions and informed judgments about the future, but this is just not going to do it for me.*

If you are the CEO of a smaller company, the scenario is different, but the challenges are similar. You will most likely be working directly with your CFO in putting together a budget and then detailed forecasts as required. You are now more directly involved in the forecasting process. You are also more involved in *gathering* some of the detail necessary to make those educated guesses that will be necessary in order to complete the budget/forecast. In other words, you are now the primary person responsible for both developing the forecasts *and* producing the forecasted results.

Here are some of the forecasting facts of life:

- In your situation, you will see firsthand the intellectual limits of some of those people being asked to provide you and your CFO with information. You will experience people who can't separate the minutiae from the whole picture. You will work with some people who have a good sense of the market and its dynamics, but whose well-meaning efforts are undermined by their total lack of ability to handle numbers. You will also see the enormous challenges involved in defining how a certain market or markets will develop, particularly when those markets are in an extremely volatile situation.

- Your sales group will be one of the numbers sources you will use. Even though you may have a finely tuned metrics system to review their sales group's unit and dollar volume forecasts, and even though your sales team should know its customers' inventory levels, the seasonality factor (if any), average weekly sell-through, as well as your customers' future business prospects, you must exercise *extreme* caution in accepting the forecasts of what your sales team thinks its customers will buy during the coming year. No matter how many training sessions on forecasting you've given your salespeople, even with the support of good software, their input should represent only one of many views you will need of the future. With the data they have, or the market they think they know, they will tend to interpret and skew their forecasts more to the upside than to the downside, unless they are playing the game of underestimating in order to look better later. There is nothing wrong with that kind of attitude, assuming they are out selling successfully with good customer face time at their customers' locations. But the fact is they will often err in judging future sales prospects. We are not talking five- or 10- percent deviations here. With the exception of locked-in customer contracts, which aren't a direct part of their forecasting activity anyway, they will more often than not take you down the path leading to unbalanced inventories, higher capital investment, and whatever else too-high or too-low sales estimates can possibly affect in the operations of your company. Unfortunately, not every industry, not every wholesaler customer group has installed effective software programs to help attack the problem of achieving more accurate forecasting by building complete databases on their customer sales and their inventory stocking performance. To really read the accuracy of your sales group forecasts, you have put yourself in a position to make a call on their judgment *in advance*.

- You must know your top customers; you must visit and talk with them about their expectations for the future. Some of your salespeople may have this kind of numerically oriented relationship, but don't be surprised if it turns out to be the exception, not the rule. Your position gives you a different quality of access to your customers' thinking. Use it often, in addition to whatever your software is delivering to you concerning historical and current customer buying behavior.

- In developing and signing off on all of the forecasts, you will be confronted with some difficult questions: Is all of this really plausible? Does it fit together? Does it make sense? Mathematically, of course, everything will add up. Hearing from your people that everything "looks good" is not good enough when judging the internal integrity of the forecast. "Best we can do" gets closer to an acceptable answer, but it can only come after you've looked at every major forecasted number and questioned its source, and the manner in which it was calculated.

Pouring over your latest budgets or forecasts, you will perhaps finally understand that you only have a thin silk thread holding your whole company construction together. That thread amounts to nothing more than a series of educated guesses—backed up by some hard external data you managed to secure, and supported by your own internal data, both historical and current.

What to do? First of all, start with something simple: During the budgeting or forecasting process, have the whole forecast, including all backup data and critical economic assumptions, stored on your computer or memory stick when you are traveling. Find a quiet place and *clear your mind* before you go at it. You are looking at what could carry your company forward at an even faster pace because of excellent forecasting, or you are looking at a possible series of speed bumps, or worse, a minefield. In the final analysis, these budget decisions are your responsibility. And you need to make them or reexamine them in peace and quiet with a *very high* concentration level.

This is the only way—unless you toss the question to your CFO—you are going to be prepared to give any a decent answer to the following question: "How did you arrive at that number?" To be followed by the most logical of follow-up questions: "Do you really believe in this number?" You will have exactly five seconds to start answering this question in a convincing and substantive fashion.

Get ready to hear this question repeatedly when you meet with your board or the owners. On the other hand, you will have already posed that question any number of times to your own people. There are two reasons you will want to keep these questions in your mind: You don't want to appear like a dummy when you can't answer them, and you have to answer them convincingly, because the success of your year and the stability of your position are directly related to your ability to answer quickly and with relevant detail. Remember, when you stand in front of your board and present these numbers for their review, the numbers will have *your* signature on them. Ditto for every latest forecast after that. You own those numbers.

Some recommendations for increasing accuracy in this area include the following:

- **The advantages of 3-D.** The people you have doing your forecasting should not only have two-dimensional experience with numbers and sources, but a three-dimensional one, meaning they have made themselves market- and operations-smart. Staring at a computer screen every day isn't going to do it, nor is sitting in meetings listening to people talk about "out there" going to suffice. They must travel repeatedly to the field and meet personally with important elements of your sales and production units, as well as your customers and other supporting vendors or external consulting staff. Selected members from your purchasing department and your operations and financial planning group are the people who should engage in this personal contact out in the field. These cannot be one-off trips; they can be infrequent, but they must, in every case, be part of a continual, professional, *in-the-market* approach to forecasting within your total group. Your discussions and debriefing sessions with them—using that gathered knowledge—will serve to improve forecasting accuracy. For your forecasting staff and the other person who carries the overall responsibility, there is *no* substitute for an understanding of the trenches.

- **It takes two to tango.** Develop a "consulting" relationship with some-one within your expanded forecasting group. You need to engage in a detailed and substantial exchange of opinions with this person on various elements of the key numbers to be forecasted. This person will not only function as a sounding board, but also must question your thinking and the steps you or you and your managers took to ar-rive at your forecasting conclusions. It is not only intelligence, a good feeling for numbers, or long years of experience in doing forecasting that you will be seeking in this person, but someone who will not shy away from telling you straight out that you are wrong or off-track—and who can back up that assessment with numbers and facts.

- **No shut-down valve on information flow.** During the times when you are not formally involved in the forecasting phases of your year, stay attuned to those key forecasting benchmarks that constitute the core of your budget and forecasts. When traveling, speaking with your customers, your sales force, colleagues, or at association meetings, remember to keep the information from these sources continually flowing to you. This strategy represents not only good prepping for the time when budget and forecasts will need to be formally devel-oped, but it will also give you added confidence in making the final call on the quality and content of your budget or forecast.

- **Maintaining the numerical integrity of your forecast.** It often hap-pens, particularly during intense discussions in the major budget-ary or forecast periods, that conflicting forecast numbers will sneak into the numbers you and your people have produced. Beware the question concerning a particular number on Page 17 of your budget and how that relates to a number in column 3 on page 189. There is very likely a connection and you must know what that connection is. Potential bridge questions of this sort call for detailed check-ing in advance of the plausibility of the numerically based critical assumptions underlying the budget, as well as cross-checking the bridges between the various numbers in the budget, in order to make sure they don't conflict with one another or cancel one another out. A correct correlation requires time and a sharp eye, as well as a fundamental understanding of the various parts of your operations and their numerical relationship to one another. Don't finesse this part of your analysis. The embarrassment that comes from totally missing these disconnections is a relatively small worry compared to the embarrassment you could experience when those conflicting numbers prove so dangerous that they cause a below-forecast performance result.

• **Your forecast is a living document.** Establish regular review periods for your forecasts. Monthly reviews after the closing of the previous month are excellent times for this exercise. Even if you don't change a thing in these meetings, you will still have formally reviewed everything included in those forecasts: the critical assumptions if they are still valid and, of course, the running year, its numbers, and their potential effect(s) on the contents of your forecasts. If you want to be master of your business, be certain that any numbers cascading through your forecasts or budgets are as accurate and accurate as they can be. To ensure that, you should be attending the key decision-making budgeting or forecast meetings in person. This is not micro-managing. And if anybody maintains that it is, then they are probably the people whose projected numbers you will want to check closely.

Good forecasting or budgeting requires hands-on and informed leadership. Those educated guesses that everyone always talks about in putting together the numbers are not enough to ensure tight operational planning and execution. It is your responsibility to take those guesses or have those guesses taken to another level.

YOUR NEXT BUDGET YEAR COULD START— AND ABRUPTLY END—AFTER Q1

Preparations for any next budget year always seem as though they have been in the process for ages. Whether there are five-year budgets, or two-year budgets, or a standard annual budget, you will always be involved in what seems to be a never-ending process of constructing a numerical framework to validate and support your company's forward strategies. This ongoing process was very familiar to you when you were manager of one of the company's divisions. Only now your job and its focus have changed. You are now the coordinator, organizer, and expeditor for everything. You are the one who has to master and have at your mental fingertips a fundamental and deep awareness of every financial way and byway of your company. You are the one that has to connect all of the dots, and to make sure that *each* company year is better than the last.

But between you as CEO and the fulfillment of this responsibility lurks a calendar problem that could cause you to miss that goal: If you blow the first quarter of your business year, you are most likely going to blow the whole year. You must find ways and means to give special emphasis and focus to the *first quarter* of the new budget year, and the planning accuracy contained in that Q1 budget.

This is critical. If that first quarter misses the goals set for it by a wide margin, it could ruin, or at least call into question, the attainability of everything you are planning to do in the remaining part of the new budget year. Depending upon how the budget and the calendar are set up, as well as possible seasonality factors, you could perhaps argue that not every first quarter has the same financial or operational importance to the company in its efforts to make the budgeted annual numbers. You could also argue that the percentage of business done in the first quarter, particularly if it is "only" 10 or 12 percent of total yearly sales, is not that important. Even if the quarter were to tank, meaning perhaps down to 75 percent below budgeted numbers, this would still only mean mathematically a 3- or 4-percent negative impact on the total budget. Unfortunately, most first quarters aren't built that way. They will generally comprise anywhere from 15 to 25 percent of your total annual sales, and if that "tank" sickness should hit before April, then you could possibly be looking at a 5- to 6-percent potential negative sales delta against your total budgeted sales numbers for the year.

There are two very troublesome byproducts of this specific problem. The *first* one is very clearly a financial or budget target problem: No normal budget contains that much resiliency or such reserves that allow it to absorb that kind of below-budget performance. There may be certain steps you can take in the remaining three quarters to compensate for this problem, but what could they possibly involve? Short-term cost reductions could include advertising expenditure reductions, personnel reductions, and program postponements, to mention a few. But what is the true cost of this? Your finely calibrated budget has lost its edge; you are now approaching, or should be potentially already in, a "save what we can" mode for the budget year. And that means the long-term view, at least as it pertains to the running year, will have started to take a backseat to short-term cost and budget exigencies, which in turn, will effectively remove a major part of the overall strength of your current annual budget.

The *second* cost is a psychological and/or motivational one. Who among your managers and operational supervisors wants to know that your new remuneration plan for them, based on performance and results contained in the budget, has now been seriously undermined by a first quarter that didn't fulfill expectations? Some of the more seriously affected will announce that the year is over before it has really begun—and such a statement will not be far from the truth. Bad motivation all around. And what will you feel like? Remember how strong you felt after your fall board meeting went so well and the media touted a great coming year for you and the company? That's gone, replaced, among other things, by major fallout in the financial community and in the media, which are definitely not going to be entranced by your badly botched first quarter. These people know how to throw up serious flak. And they aim very well.

There is only one solution to this possible dilemma: You and your management must devote the *same amount of time, focus, creativity, and attention* as you apply in planning the full budget year to a detailed planning of the first quarter. Think of the first quarter as having the same importance as the whole year. You need a detailed *week-by-week* budget plan for your first quarter, or, figuratively speaking, for your "mini-budget year."

Thirteen weeks, individually planned, *are* that important. Even *more* critical are the first several weeks of that 13-week period. Woe to the CEO or top manager who has pulled every lever in the fourth quarter of the proceeding year to get every possible sale booked before the end of the budget year. Woe to the CEO who has initiated a price increase effective January 1 of the new budget year and has not paid attention to her customers "buying out the shop" in the fourth quarter of the preceding year. Woe to the CEO who has not been watching her new product development and launch plans for the coming year's first quarter, and learns of major launch postponements several weeks before the end of the current business year, when the budget for the next year and for the planned first quarter launches are already officially locked in. And woe to the CEO who thinks that her organization needs a little bit of warm-up time at the beginning of the year to get up and running, or who rationalizes early-budget-year misses because there is still a lot of time left in the year to compensate for the missing numbers. If you are guilty of this kind of thinking, then, just for fun, do the following: Take the shortfall from the first quarter, and lay the missing numbers across the remaining nine months of the budget year. Then step back, take a close look, and ask yourself if that picture and its attainability are realistic, or represent only wishful thinking. If you were being realistically conservative in your planning, what are you being now?

The elements of the analysis required to put together a solid budget for those first 13 weeks should include the following:

- With your top management team, you reevaluate the overall relevance of your current year's budgets from a financial, tactical, and strategic point of view. Is the plan still intact and realizable?
- Dissect every single delta that occurred during the past first quarter of the year; examine the success or failure of any measures taken subsequently to reduce or eliminate any shortfalls that took place during that quarter.
- Conduct a thorough reexamination of any one-time events (big customer order, product launch, price increase, weather issues, loss of two salespeople at the end of the fourth quarter, competitive promotional moves that sapped your sell-in strength) that could have skewed those results, either positively or negatively. Further analyze the accuracy and relevance of the underlying critical assumptions and critical success factors that were built into the plan for your past first quarter.

- Construct an updated financial estimate/forecast of your over-all current year's operations and probable end-of-the-year results. Concentrate on the planning elements contained in the fourth quarter of your current year in order to be sure that the first-quarter plan numbers for next year are still achievable, and won't be negatively impacted by any major moves planned for this year's fourth quarter. This updated document will serve as the core platform for your budget planning for next year, and can be revised further until the final budget is locked in and approved for the coming year. Identify every single element of your company activities that will positively or negatively impact your company performance in the coming first quarter. Forecast one-time events and special effects that will or could eventually come into play. Particularly watch the last two weeks of the current year for possible "special effects", such as salespeople filling the pipelines to make budget and commissions, which might not be in the company's interest going forward into the new budget year. Engage in an across-the-board look at the basic and classic tools used in increasing sales volume, and how each individual tool could impact your coming first-quarter business. These would include new customer sales volume, price increases, expansion of current distribution channels and expansion into new channels, pipelining effects, geographical expansion of your business, product line expansion, one-time promotions, merger and acquisition effects, and volume of advertising dollars and their projected effect on sales levels.

This sounds like the type of work you would be doing when preparing your annual budget. There is no difference whatsoever, except in your pulse rate because you know what kind of damage a bad first quarter can cause. *Treat and prepare your first quarter as if it were your whole budget year.* Give yourself a chance to hit your year's budget numbers *without* having to transfer potential major first quarter deltas into your second, third, and fourth quarter budgeted numbers.

Running after results is a most unpleasant form of managing a business year. We all know what April is: an interesting month involving taxes, the start of spring, and baseball. April, however, is also a get real-month for CEOs. It is the month when you will know whether you still "have a year" or not.

FIVE-YEAR PLANS AND BUDGETS: OXYGEN DEPLETION AFTER TWO YEARS

It's that time again. Time to produce a realistic and numerically sound five-year plan. They are the framework that shows how you and your management intend to implement and fulfill your company's long-range mission and the goals associated with it. They legitimize the company's reason for being, and form the basis for establishing strategic goals and defining what exactly your company should be doing to reach them. Finally, they are part of the nimbus of being a forward-looking, but cautious businessperson, that is, being able to put together a sound five-year plan containing all of the appropriate and relevant priorities and strategies. The plan's existence represents something of a *Good Housekeeping* Seal for the integrity and professionalism of your leadership. What would business life be without a five-year plan?

There is nothing compared to the feeling of satisfaction one has when the plan has been completed and approved. You are quite aware that producing a sound five-year plan is not a static exercise. In order to ensure that it stays current, it must be rolled over one year later in order to maintain the integrity of the five-year time period. The trends you have used in making some of the basic assumptions used in the plan may currently be your friends, but those "friends" could very well change over a longer period of time. The trend is *not* always your friend.

If, however, such plans weren't produced and approved, would anything ever get decided? Would the whole business world fall into a deep funk of despair because there was no solid financial, numerical, and decisive approach available to "map out" the desired operational objectives and planned results? What would the economists do with themselves if they weren't constantly considering macro-economic situations and making long-term projections? Where would all of the critical assumptions go that underlie such plans? And what about all of those well-thought out critical success factors that have to be realized for the plan to have the ghost of a chance of turning into reality? If we weren't planning five years in advance, how could we give any strategic focus to the present and the future? How could we give an answer to the question of just why we are working so feverishly now, or give reasons as to what our work will mean in the future? What would the financial institutions and venture capitalists do? Suddenly lose their orientation and not be able to commit to anything? Surprisingly, that is most likely *exactly* what *would* happen. If no planning were done, we would all live from day to day with no markers, either at the beginning or at the end of our journey.

Most companies can't live without a five-year plan. And if you are in a specific business, say oil or natural gas, where the investment horizon and payback needed lie well beyond the five-year mark, you are most likely looking at 10-, 15-, or even 20-year investment stream and corresponding return assumptions, all captured in a longer-term plan. All of these plans are an omnipresent part of the corporate and economic landscape. "What's the plan?" is not just a throwaway question. It is the core of the business equation.

The fact of the matter is that you unfortunately can't really live *with* them either. In their nature and constitution, they have a basic flaw. Out beyond the two-year mark, you start to deal with a world out of focus, with a world you cannot really bring *into* focus. If you want to get a perspective on how good and reliable five-year plans really are, then the first thing you might want to do is to go back five years in your memory or take a look at your five-year plan from that point in time. What you are most likely *not* looking at is an accurate forecast of what has actually happened since that time, in spite of the best minds having been involved and careful attention having been given both to the conception, as well as to the most appropriate and profitable execution of the plan during the ensuing five-year period.

Another perspective you might want to consider would be to reconsider exactly how those who are charged with developing such plans actually go about putting them together. Not surprisingly, the first two years of the plan gel relatively quickly and can often be reasonably accurate. They contain near-term views and assumptions, and in all likelihood, numbers are already reflecting some or major parts of the plans and action programs you probably already have in progress. In fact, accuracy doesn't suffer too much because you are working with a relatively short-term view close to the present time.

But then off you go into the netherworld located beyond the two-year mark. In much of what you currently are doing, you find yourself dealing with straight-line assumptions and extrapolations, percentage relationships, past numerical experience, plug numbers, esoteric weightings, or you are pulling numbers out of the clouds. The result? A five-year plan, that is, from the point of view of reliability, actually only a two-year plan.

Through the years, you will have been involved in creating many of these types of long-range plans. But the flaw in any plan you created was always there. An example that very clearly illustrates this took place years ago at an international management conference I attended in Paris. Talk about frustration and extrapolation. Part of the task of the individual groups was to put together a first-blush, sales-and-unit, five-year plan that would then be cobbled together by management into an overall five-year plan a couple of weeks later. I would suggest that the word clueless is probably just about the nicest thing one can say about the thinking that went into this exercise. All attendees had brought their historical data, actual results in detail, and current year forecasts and budgets. Everyone had detailed information on the current and planned near-term product launches and promotional plans. Economists' reports on major economic factors and the prognosis for same were made available. Planned product drops and product changes as well as price and cost increases, were either known or assumed, based on management statements that had been included in the briefing documents. The forms to be used were clear and uncluttered; there was even space allotted for the managers to note what critical assumptions or critical success factors were included in their analysis and in the numbers finally included in the five-year plan. This was actually not the worst platform for doing the job.

The first two years of the planning exercise went smoothly. And then you could almost hear it. The groups all hit the wall at just about the same time— the two year mark. After that, the initial tightness of the planning exercise began to unravel. Despair permeated the air, but a solution was at hand. Nobody used the expression "finesse it," but just about everybody began to do what the word implied. Some fought it and tried to be as exact as possible, huffing and puffing their way through the remaining three years. The others just marched on, and did what they had to do. Out came the guesses, straight lines, averages, numbers of fictional origin, and esoteric weightings. The accuracy quotient dropped, the irrelevance factor increased, but the first draft of a five-year plan was done.

One of the participants later posed a question to management on the usefulness of such plans. The answer was illuminating, and probably as close to the truth as one will get in commenting on the worth of a five-year plan: "We want to have the most probable view of where you think the company should and will be going." *Probable*. A truer word was never spoken.

The person answering the question went on to say, "We know that it is difficult to judge the future, but this will certainly help us to put some kind of framework around where the company is, and where it could possibly land after the five years. And as far as using these plans to make our investment decisions and business plans, we will, as usual, try to be conservative. Then, ladies and gentlemen, it is up to you and your colleagues to make it happen."

Mention was also made of the need to make the five-year plan part of a rolling exercise, which would have had the salutatory effect of not condemning the plan to the desk drawer, but to making it a living instrument for the company.

What this whole exercise actually accomplished was something akin to what the CEO indicated in answering that question. That is why, in spite of their inaccuracy and increasing irrelevance after the two-year mark, five-year plans do have their place in many companies. The flaw inherent in each and every one of such plans lies simply in the nature of the beast, that is, the five-year period of time. Five-year plans are neither the planning document *sine qua non*, nor should they be tossed out with the trash because they don't really mean anything anyway, and are mostly wrong.

So what can you do to at least mitigate or minimize the problem of the flaw? The afore-mentioned "accompanying business-related assumptions" and the all-important role these factors play in your planning efforts are of critical importance. These factors would include:

- **Critical assumptions,** which serve as the basic framework of the plan. These would include, for example, the inflation rate, rate of unemployment, GDP growth, expected competitive growth, full complement of salespeople in all territories, growth in the industry or sectors in which the company was active, possible additional competitor entry into the market, price and cost increases, expected or anticipated product or service launches in the market, the cost of financing going forward, possible new government regulation or laws, or sale of assets to securing financing.

- **Critical success factors,** those being the factors that impinge directly, negatively or positively, upon the execution and successful realization of the five-year plan. They would include the following: securing appropriate and sufficient financing for a specific project or goal, the cost of that financing, the hiring of or integration into the current sales force of new additions or salespeople acquired through an acquisition, the meeting of new product launch deadlines, prompt approval of a new plant needed to produce additional quantities of product in high demand, the hiring of new marketing personnel, minimum levels of advertising and promotional funds necessary to maintain market demand, and possible cost of goods reductions that need to be obtained by the purchasing group in order to effect projected increased margin contribution.

- **The creation of subsections,** those projects or programs *within* the plan, not necessarily based on the time or year factor, each of which should have its own set of unique critical assumptions and critical success factors. The discipline necessary to put together a serious package of such individual assumptions and factors works in favor of giving the five-year plan a chance to be that which its name implies— a plan closer to the reality of what very well *could* take place during the whole full five-year period.

Do these factors or assumptions eliminate the flaw? Not necessarily, but because of their critical nature, they require a tremendous amount of thought and consideration. And that implies very strongly that they must represent strong support struts and high priorities in both your planning and execution activities. They represent the "real" five-year plan because they at least give you the foundation and benchmarks necessary to map a plausible scenario of growth for your company during the next five years. And you, by seeing the value of the five-year plan, and constructing that plausible map, have strongly contributed to setting up your company, so that your employees know what they are striving for and fighting to do.

However, because they are in the type of business that allows them to do so, some companies have looked at all of this and decided to operate on a rolling two-year cycle. There's good reason to do so. In today's world, things change so rapidly that two years have become what five years were several decades ago. If you want to take your company down this particular road, you would be making a decision that is in no way unreasonable. But then, of course, you would have to change the prevailing mindset of the many different "constituencies" in your world. The thinking of many is that covering anything shorter than five years doesn't prepare the company for many of the possible scenarios out beyond the two-year mark that could impinge upon the long-term success of the company. That kind of thinking automatically brings us back to the critical assumptions and critical success factors and the *conditio sine qua non* role they play in neutralizing part of the negative effects of the flaw, while providing a strong framework for that supposedly necessary five-year plan.

If you do in fact decide to use or continue to use the five-year plan approach and you have your planning assumptions locked in all the way down to the last comma, you still could miss hitting your objectives. It happens, so here a final bit of advice: After the five years are over, do yourself a favor and don't take too close a look at the last three years of the plan compared to actual results.

Whether the results are over or under plan, relax. You're in good company.

Key Priorities

- Solid historical and market data, knowledge of the strengths and weaknesses of your company, and educated guesses about critical factors impacting your company's future represent some of the key factors in proper forecasting. There are many steps you must take to improve your chances of hitting the marks you have set. One is making sure your people understand the world they are looking at, and how your company works within that world.
- In 13 weeks, your year could be done before you have really started to get up some steam. Treat and plan your first quarter as you treat and plan your whole budget year. And avoid a potentially large delta you might be forced to chase after for the rest of the budget year.

- Five-year plans have two parts: the period you can see pretty clearly and plan accordingly for (the first two years) and then the rest. Planning the latter, unless you secure that plan with well-considered critical assumptions and critical success factors, will have you and your people using their best finessing techniques. Nice recipe for big misses and potential disaster.

Chapter 9

ANTICIPATING, MITIGATING, AND AVOIDING OPERATIONAL MELTDOWN

While you may be a total professional, your operational abilities won't usually include a highly developed warning system, giving you advanced notice of when things are about to "fall out of bed." You need to recognize and neutralize those dangers—and their sources—before they do their damage. The worst are those that have the word "surprise" written all over them. While nearly everybody likes surprises, operationally, they have *no place* in your company. Here's what can happen when you don't provide for the correct counter-measures in *advance* of any approaching storm.

THE FOURTH QUARTER BLUES: NO COASTING TO THE FINISH LINE THIS YEAR

Addressing a big miss in your quarterly results during the year can be a major test of your leadership abilities. But what if you are in the middle of the fourth quarter of your current budget year, and you already know the quarter is done? Even worse, you suspect it could possibly take your whole year down.

It is the middle of October, a warm Indian summer afternoon, nice weather befitting your current good year—and good mood. But your CFO called this morning while you were out and left a cryptic message concerning some problems with the fourth quarter estimates. "We have some issues. Can we meet?"

You think *uh oh*. This could be bad news because this is someone who doesn't waste time calling to chit-chat. If he is referencing newer versions of fourth quarter estimates, then you know he is probably also talking about the full operating year as well.

Ten days ago, you had your latest end-of-year current-year estimate in your pocket, and it was excellent. You met with your full board to give final details on where the year would end (very pleasant lunch afterwards), you had several calls with the analysts (they were enthusiastic), put some happy notes on the company Intranet on how great the current year is shaping up, and gave a leading business paper an interview on how you go about smoothing out large negative and positive demand movements in your market. Nothing was standing in the way of a rousing, end-of-the-year corporate parade.

And now this.

Fast forward now to the same time the next day: You sit alone in your office, the weather outside still warm and sunny, but inside in your office a number of things have rained on your parade. All you can think of are the questions and comments your CFO posed at yesterday's meeting on key elements of the latest forecast for the quarter and the year:

- "Remember when we discussed those developing bad numbers from Subsidiary A and D last quarter and decided not to get excited...?"
- "Some of our people missed some things when they looked at..."
- "Two of our largest customers want to cancel their last two orders for the year. How do we want to react here?"
- "Remember the ABC company and that dangerous accounts receivable position we have recently built up with them...?"

- "It appears we are going to have to take back tens of thousands of that new product we delivered in the last four months due to a component failure..."
- "We will have to give all of our customers immediate credit for the product returned because we won't have replacements for several months..."

Plan A, which is finishing the year on a positive note, is effectively out the window. Plan B needs to be put on the table quickly and executed even more quickly. But you don't have a Plan B because this wasn't supposed to happen.

You call the usual meetings and find prescriptive changes to try to cushion the nasty effects. Some of this could have happened to any company and couldn't be foreseen—right? You pose to yourself the thoroughly uncomfortable question about how you are going to explain all of this to the same audience you gave an entirely different message to several weeks ago.

Meanwhile, you and your CFO have tried to blunt at least part of the damage by moving things around within the remaining scope of the budget, or by eliminating or postponing certain planned expenditures. It is not enough. Five minutes ago, your CFO sent you an email with the new top and bottom line projected results: The year is doomed. The "bills" for past misdeeds and false forecasts are on their way, and they will be paid. One of those bills concerns a question relating to your grip on the company and its day-to-day operation. Within a 10-day span, there is an almost night-and-day difference in forecasted company results for the quarter and the year. Maximum *uh-oh*.

It is not necessarily so that everything bad only happens in the fourth quarter. There are also surprises in the first, second, and third quarter, but the year is still running, and you still have time to react and cushion the effects. Also, some of these surprises will hurt relatively less when your company is riding a big sales increase, growing its margins, or has pricing power along with industry growth under its feet. But what company is constantly and continually on that kind of a roll? If your company is not, such surprises hurt big every time, and they will hurt the worst in the fourth quarter. If your personal mistakes are the cause, such surprises can represent nothing more and nothing less than a potential career killer. Your tenure has just met a reality called "the end of the year."

Avoid the chaos and problems caused by surprises in the fourth quarter by knowing the probable causes:

- Bad forecasts
- Bad estimates
- Critical assumptions proving to be false across the board
- Operating from best case scenarios
- Critical success factors not adequately executed
- Postponement of negative financial consequences
- A lack of metrics providing early warning of potential problems
- Negative stifling of company personnel's attempts to communicate threatening or imminent bad news to top management
- Past retribution directed toward company personnel for badly handled programs
- Rationalizing the warnings coming from the market and/or large customers about demand fall-off
- Believing all economists and their forecasts
- Putting sales to your customers ahead of watching those same customers' aging metrics and their overall dollar amount receivables (bankruptcy risk)
- Problems in key areas such as inventories or bad debts or warranty issues
- Believing your customers forecasts without corroborating and double-checking them for credibility and realistic thinking

There could also be deeper reasons for you and the company getting caught up in this kind of a bind. What was the prevailing philosophy in the company that painted white what should have been painted black? What possible measures could have been taken in order to avoid some of the more preventable problems from ever seeing the light of day?

The problem lies in the nature of the beast.

In spite of the rapidly changing character of your industry and the economy, you will most likely have put a tight corset around the current budget year. Neither wiggle room nor many reserves were built in. Unfortunately, hope often springs eternal when planning a new budget year. Do you need show some progress, show some growth? Was that the mindset at budget time?

That budget corset may have gotten tighter during the course of the current year because of the early surprises that popped up and had to be resolved. Those surprises cost most of the reserves you may have built into your budget, thus leaving you with little or no room or time for you to maneuver in—or turn things around.

Constant knowledge of possible potholes and pitfalls.

It is possible that you already knew some of these problems and had appraised their potential effects on your quarterly and full-year forecasts. But after analyzing the respective situation and possible up-and-down risks associated with those problems, you and your management team chose to come down on the side of "we have our plans and these things will be taken care of by then." In addition, no one talked about new issues that could blindside the company and your management so late in the game. The risks were there, but you took a close look at everything—or so you thought. Or maybe you did consider and reserve for some of them, and you still came up with an excellent year—on paper. Apparently you didn't catch them all, however, or perhaps you didn't correctly assess them all, so you had no cushion to absorb their surprise effect.

What you hear is not what you might get.

Some of your people will be guilty of the most elementary of mistakes: thinking they are giving you and your management what they think *you want to hear*. Unless you have made specific your wish to have forecasting done in a conservative fashion, and have backed up that demand with specific reductions in the numbers submitted for review and inclusion in the latest forecast, your people will tend to come in on the high side with their estimates.

Making lists and practicing intensive due diligence.

Did anybody make a list of those specific risks and problem areas that had been identified in the second and third quarter in each operational area of the company, along with some assumptions about possible sleepers? Did anybody set up a committee to review (at least bi-weekly) each of those risk areas and the steps taken to make sure they stay where they are? Did anybody think about contingency plans? Did anyone take care of the "follow through"?

The income factor.

In most companies, there is an "everybody shares" approach to bonus payments. Some exceptions exist, of course, usually relating to specific contracts with individuals or groups within a whole company or financial institution. Is it possible that, due to the bad surprises in the preceding quarters, the general tenor in the company had become something approaching the following statement? *No chance to save the year with all of these problems and costs involved. Might as well let the year run its course. No bonus this year.*

The dream-on factor.

This is a cousin of the income factor. Many people in management positions tend to delude themselves, looking at the forecasted/budgeted numbers on paper that indicate good bonus numbers at the end of the year. They will more or less stay with those numbers and estimates, even when they know that certain risks exist that essentially negate any chance they may have of ever seeing a bonus. What they hoped for will never comes to pass, but at least they feel good for most of the year before reality sets in.

Aren't these factors just part of doing business, and won't there always be a certain amount of what the French call *gaspillage* (waste)? Obviously, it's easier for you to answer all of that with a big yes. You can conclude it is simply the way the organizations function: Yes, surprises happen every year, and many in the fourth quarter. Yes, because you think there is really not much you can do about eliminating those problems because they are systemic and macro-economic, and therefore cannot be totally eliminated. Yes, because while you recognize the dangers and tried to account for their effects, it is not your fault, and who can make you responsible for this kind of thing? Get real. Plenty of people will look askance at you because of this problem.

You're thinking it might be time to invite everyone to your version of a Category 5 hurricane, giving them an intimate understanding of what a storm can mean in a company that has just hit the wall. While it could ease your stress, it is definitely a no-no. In addition, don't be tempted to go down the path of citing externally generated problems or "corporate life is like that" reasons as the cause of your fourth quarter surprise. You know the real reasons, and they didn't just come in from the cold. They were already there.

So how do you get your arms around this situation upriver (Quarters I, II, and III) as a way of protecting yourself and your company downriver (Quarter IV) and then do it every year going forward?

Begin with the standard stuff. You know there are always going to be things in your company that are not exactly well-organized or being executed properly. In your budgeting, you can certainly adapt a cautious stance. In the budget package to be sent out to all departments and divisions, your CFO can certainly list the macro-economic and micro-economic benchmarks your people should be using in doing their individual budget work, and make sure they are correctly and accurately considered in the ensuing budget work. This is standard stuff.

In spite of such efforts, including your warnings of the frailty of hope and stories about disasters, a lot can happen in a year, and it usually does. You need to do something more.

The most appropriate and most effective thing you can do is to *institutionalize* the assumption that, whatever you or the company does, some things are going to go awry during any budget year. Weird idea? Not at all. It means you must create an instrument that can identify, quantify, and qualify every single operational or financial risk showing up on the company radar screen as being potentially dangerous, and neutralize them (if possible) before they get into the late stages of your current year.

Depending upon the size of your company, the overall regulatory situation, and your board's involvement in this area, you will most likely have established some formal, internal risk-management process in your company. Its orientation will most likely be skewed toward identifying, isolating, and taking corrective measures to mitigate any major financial or organizational problems for the company, middle- to long-term. However, you need to add a more short-range setting to the "risk search" radar you are using to look for possible operational danger and risk. In the situation at hand, operational mishaps that could threaten the fourth quarter results, as well as those of the whole year, while certainly risks, are not generally in the same league compared to those risks that could threaten the very integrity and/or existence of the company. This doesn't mean you should underestimate the relevance of the smaller risks because of their relative lack of danger.

In guarding against such mishaps, you don't need to create a separate risk management group or committee. Use what you already have. Create a separate group within the overall risk management activity whose charge it is to consistently and continually "sweep" for potential risks to the company and its benchmark goals *within the current budget year.* Have it work with the respective operational groups affected to minimize these immediate potential problems or concerns. By definition, then, the charge of this group would go well beyond the day-to-day, straight-forward, controlling function as handled by the controller or the CFO himself within the Finance Department.

In populating the committee, you should install some of the same team that worked on and prepared the final budget, perhaps two or three people, as well as yourself and at least one representative from your controlling department. Your CFO should be a permanent member and chairman *pro tem* of this committee, just as he is involved in the overall responsibility for the total risk management function.

The tasks of this subcommittee during your operating year would be simple:

1. On a continuing basis, and in coordination with relevant operational managers, identify every single potential major sales, cost, or profit risk, operation by operation, division by division, discipline by discipline.

2. Coordinate with top management and the relevant operational managers to find effective remedies and solutions to reduce or eliminate a particular identified risk.

3. Employ follow-up controls to make sure that every specific risk-abatement or risk-elimination solution is executed in a timely and effective manner in order to minimize or completely eliminate any remaining risk or risks *for the current year.*

Depending upon the discipline or operation involved, minimum standards would have to be established for any operational problem to qualify as a risk, and therefore be subject to continued committee attention. The committee would start its work after the January results were available and continue that work until December of each year. Action proposals would be submitted each month to the committee on the various concerns uncovered, and the solutions currently being applied to them.

Functional and disciplinary authority for their operations, as well as the responsibility to neutralize or eliminate the identified risks, would still rest with the respective department and division heads, but the committee, in its supportive and analytical role, would keep book and provide an overview of any and all risks facing the company. A central risk-overview unit and clearinghouse would perhaps be another good way to describe its function and responsibilities. Monthly reports would be issued by this group whereby the meeting schedule (monthly under normal conditions), would depend upon the time of year, the number of risks involved, the immediate or secondary gravity of those risks, and the need to eliminate them before the end of the current year.

ON SUMMER SOLDIERS AND SUNSHINE PATRIOTS: HUBRIS DOES HAVE AN ANTIDOTE

Not surprisingly, there are also those times when there are really no bad quarters, nor are there any disastrous fourth-quarter surprises. Year after year, the sales and profit curves show only one direction: up. Life is really good.

You are looking at the performance charts of your company and smiling broadly. Demand for company products is at a new high, new product introductions have exceeded expectations, average contribution margins are running well over budget, pricing power remains strong due to continued attractiveness and uniqueness of the company products, the new product pipeline is full, competition has had little or no effective counter-measures to combat the increases in your market share, the balance sheet shows a minimum of debt, the latest acquisition to provide some profit and product balance to your company's market position has turned into a real jewel, cash generation is 17 percent over budget for the first quarter of the current budget year, last week's national sales conference was the best ever, the new plant construction is on schedule for completion early next year with new production efficiencies planned, profit growth exceeds an annualized rate of more than 30 percent, the board has just approved the bonuses to be paid for the previous fiscal year (best ever), and do not forget, the company has just been voted into the Top 100 of the Fasting-Growing Companies in America. What could possibly go wrong here?

In the short-term, probably not very much. You should still be seriously worried. In all that is going on now lies hidden the sweet seduction of continued success, and the enormous danger of hubris that success of this sort can produce.

Worse yet, you know that the people you watch and see every day are not mentally and operationally prepared for stagnation or for a downturn in the fortunes of the company. They don't know anything but the roll. You know that a number of them would most likely resign if the company's fortunes changed, especially those who have never known anything but increasing sales and profits, and bonus payments or stock options. This type of arrogance and Teflon thinking should be an anathema to you and your way of operating in such an environment.

You think often of an example you cite in your internal company marketing and strategic planning discussions. You might say, "The strategy we are currently using to get us to the top of our industry or field is not going to be the same strategy we will use to stay at the top once we get there. Nor will it be the same strategy we would use were we to fall back down the slope from where we came." What you are really saying is that the company has to be prepared for all kinds of weather. But who is listening to any of this? The sun is shining and its summer.

You continue by reminding them that because the company is at the top, you are no longer chasing the number one position. Now you are trying to maintain and build on that top position. "We must be careful not to tumble down the mountain," you tell them. They nod as they figure out how to spend the expected bonuses. Unfortunately, the roar of success is just too loud.

Your concern about your people not being able to handle anything but hot growth should encompass this thought: The people who have played a key role in propelling the company to the top may, in fact, not even be suitable or capable of handling a situation that is anything but top. In short, the supposed people strengths of your company may need to be shifted dramatically in their weighting and makeup when you go into a period of no growth or falling sales and margins.

If true, you have a right to be worried.

But how do you get your company and people to run "hot and cold" at the same time? How do you set the right temperature and the right strategy for both worlds? What preventive measures or actions must you take? How do you know who can handle a slowdown or change in company fortunes, and who can't? How do you take away some of the ill-effects of hubris, still keep everyone motivated, and keep the stakeholders believing that their investment has long-term legs?

An important part of the answer lies in the mental and attitudinal area: You must work to ensure that your people recognize the fact that downturns *do take place*. It is your responsibility to temper and reduce hubris with stark realism.

Before you get involved in the mental side of the equation, there are, of course, many strategic and operational solutions that can cushion any loss of momentum or downturn in sales. They could primarily involve taking your company into other areas of the economy through vertical, horizontal, or lateral acquisitions. Acquisitions, however, are never easy, and effective operational integration takes time. They are also costly, have a dilutive effect on the outstanding stock (if done on a non-cash deal basis), and usually produce more problems than originally anticipated. At times, they also can directly—and sometimes negatively—impact the course of your company's rhythm of growth. The plus side of this: Your people would all be out there working hard to get back on the overall success track and the good life. A dose of old-fashioned operational difficulties, and an insolvable situation every once in a while provides a sobering influence upon any company.

In addition, building up a major cash position and investing those funds would also belong on the list of things to do to protect the company. Extreme caution in the conception and approval of long-term capital commitments with the financing not yet locked in would also fall under the category of necessary and prudent caution. If there is a need for borrowing, you are now bargaining from a position of strength, so for long-term capital commitments, you can now negotiate more favorable terms for your financing. Another area where you should be careful is in not locking in too many long-term, high-dollar commitment contracts to key personnel. Should no investments be planned in the short- or middle term, then any reserves resulting from retained earnings could be used to pay down any debt you may have on the balance sheet from the years of building the company. Another good solid look at your company, its strengths and weaknesses, and its forward strategy would also be appropriate.

One step you can take during the time you spend evaluating the ability of the company to absorb a downturn is this: Be absolutely sure your company and its talent are not all of the sunny-side-up variety. This means ensuring that the company hires people who not only are all-round talents in their specific specialty, but people who are realists, who have been through the mill, who have been on both sides of the street and survived, both job and environment-wise, in both good and bad times.

That doesn't remove or mitigate the problem of hubris you currently have. The story goes that JP Morgan was once asked what stocks would be doing the next day when the market opened. His answer was simple. "They will fluctuate." And so it is with companies, industries, and the economy. Here they are called cycles, and hubris doesn't survive a down cycle, nor do a number people who emotionally and professionally collapse when involved in a change from a high-flyer situation to the necessity of having to scramble. They don't know how to do it; they can't handle it.

When one observes such people moving from a set of highs to a set of lows, they seem to go through a change of personality. They lose their *joie de vivre*, but what is even more alarming is the fact that they seem to lose the edge they had when they were driving the company forward. Others in the company are perhaps also beginning to recognize the fact that these people no longer have the specific skill maturity that is needed to stop the downward trend and redirect the company and its fortunes upwards. This is fallout from a potentially bad situation, which you don't need. Patience, deep experience in similar difficult times in the past, living with uncertainty and stress, and accepting and living with less financial "pop" for a period of time are the management attributes that are required.

If you haven't had this approach in recruiting, and trouble looms, a certain amount of thrashing about among your existing team will start to take place when, in actual fact, the focused and experienced approach would be the more appropriate solution. *Accentuate the short-term* will become the mantra for everything your existing team does. All the while, the forces potentially driving your managers and the company down continue to increase in strength and tempo.

You need to know that your organization has the depth and breadth of operational strength, as well as the conviction to be able to live through any downturn in its fortunes and survive, and you need to know who among your managers is most likely going to be able, in a mature and effective fashion, to adapt, contribute, and survive *whatever* the company situation.

You need a forum for this kind of detective work.

An appropriate solution would be to spend some time during your quarterly or half-year strategic planning sessions on playing the game of "What If?" This type of exercise can be useful in three ways: It is what you are there for anyway; It brings front and center a discussion on the possible problems the company could face if a downturn took place, as well as initiating a discussion relative to how the company would react to master this kind of situation; It provides a means for you to get a different and useful "take" on each member of your top management team.

As part of your overall strategic meeting, reserve two full days for this exercise. Do not have this meeting on your company premises. Whether you do it in a big group or smaller groups doesn't matter. Of greater relevance are the reaction and actions of the group(s), the contents of the discussion, and answers to the following key sets of questions, which you would pose in separate sections at the beginning of the session:

1. What is it that distinguishes us from the rest of our industry and what, as we move forward, are our particular strengths, organizationally, operationally, and in financial terms? Do we have any weaknesses that threaten the company's well-being in the future? What threats do we see that could possibly endanger this happy situation? Classic SWOT.

2. What strengths would remain on the list if the company entered into a period of stagnation or falling sales and profits? What kinds of problems would the weaknesses we identify cause us if we allowed their continued existence without taking the time to eliminate or neutralize them before a potential downturn hits us? Is how we are currently structured as a company, both personnel and organization wise, adequate to meet potential downturn challenges that could face us? Could our weaknesses become magnified in a downturn situation? Are we, as a company and as individuals, experienced enough or realistic enough to be able to weather a serious deterioration in our affairs, and possible period of lower-than-normal results? Do we have any attitudinal problems that are standing in our way?

3. Do we currently have the right people in the right jobs, for both summer and winter? Do we have backup, should any fail or fall by the wayside? In what condition is our succession policy, and what characteristics do these people have that would make them suitable or not suitable for a crisis situation? If we do not have that depth in our team, what do we specifically need to do about it? Are we hiring the right people for both the good and the bad times?

During the two day seminar, provide a case study of such a crisis situation to the groups, and have them make recommendations on how to prevent the company in question from falling down or being seriously weakened, and perhaps failing in the face of specific long-term crisis. Above all, observe who leads the group discussion and in presenting the findings of the group. What you are looking for here is some solid and three-dimensional thinking.

The substantive matters relating to the discussion are useful, but what should really get your interest is the quality and intensity (or lack thereof) of the discussion among your individual top managers, and the care they put into developing answers during the whole two-day event. You are looking for attitudinal reactions, seriousness of thought, appreciation of the situation and problem at hand, and apparent maturity in handling a crisis situation. Be assured, you will find these attributes in some, but unfortunately, you will also find them lacking in others.

Take careful note of who does what, who says what, and how it is said or presented. Generally, the ones who take you and the questions seriously and understand you are sending them a signal to reflect on darker times are also the people who are not only performing well with the company's rapid growth, but most likely they will also be the major players in your organization in trying times, should they come.

By using this exercise, you will be able to create an interesting and handy opportunity to help you in your search to seek out and then mold the "right temperature" and balanced attitude for your company and your people.

After the session, create an ad hoc group of those who performed well at the strategy sessions. Charge them with the problem and issue solution phase of the exercise, using the information gathered during the exercise.

With this kind of meeting correctly managed, you will have created four specific advantages for your company. You will have: contributed to strengthening, as well as protecting, your company's position; identified those things and matters you have to take into consideration to prepare for an eventual downturn; sent a strong signal to your managers, without even saying it that it is time to turn down the heat a little; started to identify those managers who most likely possess the talent to effectively carry the load in that kind of a situation, should it ever arise.

THE BAD NEWS: YOU NEED IT YESTERDAY

In all the discussion about bad quarters and bad surprises, there is always someone whose job it is to officially transport the news. Whistle blowing or bringing the bad news days is hard and dangerous work. The runner who arrived in Athens 2,600 years ago to announce that the war had been lost didn't exactly have a rewarding experience when he arrived. He didn't survive. Nobody likes to hear that things are going poorly, or that they have already effectively gone down, perhaps even permanently. We are not talking about things you may learn about in your reporting and controlling package, in reports from your division heads, from the daily calls you receive concerning operational mishaps or delays, in the occasional sales force field report you may read, or from your lawyers writing you about the latest case you might have to put into the loss column.

This is about the things you *haven't* heard about, or don't know exist as problems or dangers. This is about those matters your people are well aware of that, but you don't have a clue about, or where you may have been totally missing the warning signals. These are exactly the things you *must* have knowledge of if you are going to do your job successfully. Occasionally, you have had someone take you aside and tell you something, but those really were smaller issues, you thought, and so a small opportunity was lost to train your people to talk to you or your managers about such things. Odd, because you are most likely one of those who believe that there are more bad news things than good things going on in the company that you don't know about. How right you are.

Perhaps you don't know how to break down the barrier between yourself and your people and encourage them to come to you with important information, or you have broadcast the wrong message in the past: not listening, criticizing, rationalizing, or allowing one of your managers to react with retribution toward the message carrier when informed about bad news. Perhaps you have erred even worse by not doing a leadership check on yourself that might show that *you* are the one blocking your people from bringing the bad news, because they think you don't care and have no interest in knowing what is really occurring. That creates fear of you and your reaction.

Everything that is going wrong or could possibly go wrong should have a clear shot at being heard and heeded by you. Those providing that kind of information should be welcomed. Your people should know that what they are doing will be appreciated as a positive contribution to the company and its welfare. They should know you will never call them a stupid alarmist or set the end date of their employment because they came to talk to you.

Occasionally, if the company has a suggestion box, you might find a slip of paper inside with some alarming news on it. There is, however, a major shortcoming to the use of these boxes: The author will most likely have chosen to remain anonymous, and so any chance of getting substantial information on the issue is limited. You know about something being wrong; there is some bad news out there in a particular department or division, but all of it could be well-hidden.

So how do you go about finding out where the bad news is and where it potentially is already staging? How do you create the best possible environment and attitude in your company, where this information will be brought to you in a positive fashion, and where the people bringing it will want to appear personally and talk to you about it, and feel good and positive about it?

First, do not develop a rush-rush program and berate your people on the Intranet about your need to know anything that could hurt the welfare of "your" company. Many people will not want to come to you or other people who are responsible and talk about these things because they involve "tattling"—and you know what the other kids do to tattlers. The only way to get people past that perception is to routinely exhibit a management-leadership style that involves no retribution or disdain for your people taking a risk that seems to be in the best interests of the company.

I once spoke to the Director of Product Development for a major U.S. corporation, a smart and very organized fellow. Above all, this person was a loyal employee and often thought about how his development work fit into the overall scheme of things, and whether or not the company was in fact developing its product in the most efficient and market-oriented fashion. He knew the bad news from A to Z and yet, instead of his superiors, he was telling me, an outsider, about all of this.

He related the number of things he had seen that were going or had gone wrong in product development, questioned cost overruns, excess time for taking care of second-tier issues, and acrimonious meetings where people were beaten down when they volunteered an opinion that was not in sync with that of top management. He criticized the continual lack of focus on the part of key people involved in the product project teams. He bemoaned the fact that the products he had under his care would not, in many cases, meet the minimum performance requirements established for them at the beginning of the project, in spite of his warnings. The whole department was going nowhere fast, and it was taking the company along with it.

He was particularly disturbed by what he saw as dangerous and potentially serious technical problems. He related that he had spoken in the past with the senior executive of the company and, every time he did, had gotten nothing more than a bloody nose for his efforts. Over and over again, he had attempted to transport the bad news to the head of the company, and every time he came back to his office with nothing to show for it. I asked him how he then lived with that kind of situation. His answer: "I do my job, and I keep my head down. I don't make waves anymore."

How very sad—and how destructively dangerous—this situation is. The company for whom this person still works continues to suffer through a deteriorating market position. Is this an exception, or does this happen often? Unfortunately, the truly tragic part of all of this is that the latter is the more appropriate answer.

Creating an environment where bad news will be brought to the fore is neither an overnight process, nor one that can be solved with a patchwork of temporary fixes. This reorientation of your company think on this issue is, time-wise, a long, slow build with the need for constant and positive reinforcement of the belief and trust on the part of your employees and your executives that you really do *want to know* the bad news. You want people to walk through your door, or that of your managers, and talk about the potential negatives coming at you and your company. Not to tattle, but to talk about things they are having problems solving, or where they are losing the battle to stop the bad effects of something particular. You intend to meet them *more than halfway* and, in a professional manner, dialogue with them on the causes and the possible solutions.

Even if you have to swallow hard because the information they bring to you is anything but good, respect their intentions, and honor their bravery. No retribution. It's especially bad if the news doesn't make you look good. Worse yet, you recognize that it may be too late to really do something about what they have told you. It is not easy to handle, but necessary in every way.

Changing the way in which your people deal with the bad news is not an overnight proposition. You will need a solid, long-term program to achieve this kind of situation where your people deep inside the company will feel free and encouraged to offer you their perception on what is not working or advise you of dangers they see in a serious and factual manner.

Seek serious and clear information.

The first and most important thing you have to do is to tell your personnel exactly what you are looking for. Do it continually, and at every opportunity, in the clearest of terms. This doesn't mean a two sentence pronouncement or such on your part ("I need better information"), but a major and detailed policy statement directed at all personnel in the company. For such a serious matter, a personal letter is always better than your blog.

This is a letter you might want to spend some time writing, because essentially you are communicating your business philosophy, underlining your leadership style, and specifying the standards and support you expect from everyone in the company. The overall tone of the message in your letter should be: "Tell me if there is something that could hurt all of us. You all know how important this type of information is. This company will not take offense at bad news, or you for bringing it to our attention." In your letter, you should also make sure that you delineate and detail the procedures for company personnel to approach you or their immediate superior formally, as well as informally. You may mention that, while anonymous letters are nice, they really don't help. You also need to make clear the distinctions between tattling and serious endeavors that would help the company by providing relevant and timely information on things going awry. Avoid creating the impression that you are asking them to do something that their colleagues would find unacceptable. Close your letter by being explicit in explaining how you and the company will react to this kind of information and knowledge, and in what positive ways you would see such knowledge being used. If you couch the letter in terms of the "greater good," (that is, company, jobs, financial strength, and security of market position), then you will most likely start to get some of the information you need. Caveat: The correct assumption is that you will get more useful information than you have had in the past. Unfortunately, you *won't* get all of it.

This is not a one-man show.

Make sure that you don't create the impression that it is only you who will be receptive and understanding when informed of some bad news. This is a total team effort and approach. If you don't have your whole management team fully and completely behind you on this, then you are finished before you even start. The letter, as well as any follow-up meetings and informal discussions and reminders, must strongly emphasize the fact that you and management are united in this "information open door" approach. Unfortunately, you will find that even though you make this initial effort and reinforce the message, everything important that is happening will not be communicated to you. That is a fact of life. But it is also a fact of life that you will have made it a mantra of your administration, that it will be clear to all concerned that the top management of your company is on board, and that there is no question concerning your personal position and intended impact on the situation. That is far better than the "nothing" that was there before.

Show you mean what you say and you say what you mean.

Put the proof on the table that you are serious and that the company will conduct itself as declared. That means *every time*, and with no exceptions for anyone. Make one exception, and you will undermine what you are trying to create. Be very careful about how you proceed if you are confronted with some egregious tattling. This sort of thing is unacceptable. While the tattling might contain some unfortunately true information, your position must be to find this information in a totally different fashion, using established company practices and benchmarks. Giving tattlers their due is the best way to create the worst of toxic brews in your company, namely mutual distrust.

As you work on strengthening your new policy, let's assume a situation where the employee or the department has clearly made a mistake that is, or could be, costly for the group or the company. There are two issues you must address: First, be sure that employee receives thanks for his information, but at the same time, understands his mistakes and has learned from them. You may even have to warn such employees in written form about this, but use tones that are positive. Build them up, don't tear them down.

Second, ensure that the problem itself *is taken care of appropriately and professionally*. This may also involve other people who might or might not know how that information found its way to you, and who were also perhaps involved in causing the bad news. Not a neat situation, but certainly a situation where good and fair leadership will be called for, and where you personally will most likely have to get involved.

It is of paramount importance that the people coming to you your management team not only see and experience the company in a listening mode, but that they also *experience* you and the company *actively* moving to correct or adjust those things that have gone out of whack. These people will only really think you are serious and view your actions as credible when they are backed up by your action and you seeking solutions. They will ask, "Has anything changed?" If it has, they will continue to pass on the bad news with the good news.

One of the smartest things you can do with these people, both those who came with the news, and those who were involved in creating the problem, is to *include* them in working jointly with you and/or your managers and others to solve the problem, and create the preconditions necessary so that it never happens again. They will sense that they are still valuable and valued members of the organization, and respond accordingly. If, however, you only thank them and then push them aside, you are very quickly going to be right back at square one.

Nobody likes bad news, but you know you need much more than the good news. Proceed carefully and appreciate your people when they come to you. And then watch how they reward you in kind.

Key Priorities

- No rousing end-of-the-year parade this year. Your fourth quarter has just tanked. You need to take a series of appropriate measures, including identifying every single possible danger to your budget year upstream to enjoy a late-autumn/early winter coast to the finish line downstream.

- The party just goes on and on. The company is on a roll. Hubris rules the day. You need to get your company running "hot and cold" at the same time. And you need to know who can handle the volatility should a change in your company's fortunes ever take place. Get yourself a forum for this work and then observe and observe.

- If you have the bad news on the table, it is already too late to do anything about it. Create the prerequisites for your people to want to come to you and tell you what is going wrong in your company—*before* the bad news does its damage.

CONCLUSION

The idea for this book came to me while flying from San Francisco to Chicago. During that flight, I compiled a list of issues and situations that I felt most frequently confronted CEOs and, at times, confounded us in the daily practice of our profession. You have just finished reading about the ways and means I feel are most appropriate in order to successfully navigate many of those situations I view as most troublesome or challenging.

The section contents, including recommendations and insights, reflect my 30-year experience as a CEO. While at times you may disagree with me in regard to the issues I have selected, or to the manner in which I suggest they be resolved, I believe there are certain common principles of leadership that must be part of each and every one of the solutions or approaches I propose in this book. The position of the CEO today is a lonely one, beset with problems and opportunities

215

from all points of the compass. What appear to be major prerequisites for CEO success are the necessity for you to:

- Know *exactly* who and what you are, what you stand for, and will fight for.
- Approach the leadership of your employees with toughness, but also compassion and understanding while, at the same time, acknowledging good performance.
- Ensure that your company has *defined* itself and what it does in a manner that garners broad acceptance among your constituents— that is, the board, the shareholders, your employees, and your business environment.
- Be *personally engaged* in forming, shaping, and building your team, and also in helping it successfully execute your company's tactical and strategic plans.
- Not only *communicate* clearly and convincingly, but also to *listen* effectively.
- Use your knowledge of *details as a powerful tool* to lead your company.
- Be *business smart*, constantly on the lookout for hidden dangers and possible minefields that could hurt or impair your ability to keep the company on a smooth path.
- Use your power to *shape events and policies*, particularly when no consensus can be reached among your management on a particular issue.
- *Temper* the "extremes" that can occur within your company *with foresight and diplomacy*.
- Understand, in a profound and in-depth manner, the *potential and limits* of the sales resources available to you and your company.
- Build solid and, where appropriate, *personal* relationships with your customers and vendors.
- Set up your organization in a manner that *encourages the timely capture* of bad news that could have the potential to seriously endanger your company.
- Understand that the only person who will really be interested in *protecting your job* is you.

It is my hope that this book will contribute to reducing or eliminating the sometimes sharp edges of those pitfalls you may encounter during your CEO business journey. At the same time, I hope it increases your personal enjoyment factor, as well as your ability to insert your competence and farsightedness into your company's efforts to be the "best of the best."

INDEX

About the Author

Neil Giarratana combines experience as a top executive in six different countries with sterling academic credentials. He can articulate his insights with humor and precision in English, German, and French.

The author spent more than 30 years living and working in Europe—Germany, Austria, England, Switzerland, and France—in addition to his recent status as CEO in the United States. Since the age of 38, he has served as chief executive of several major American company subsidiaries in Europe, as well as German companies operating in Europe and/or around the world.

During the many years in Germany, he was a sought-after commentator for the *Frankfurter Allgemeine Zeitung* and *Manager Magazine*, Germany's leading newspaper and business management magazine, respectively. He is an active member of the President's Circle of the Chicago Council for Global Affairs, participating in both smaller formal dinner discussions as well as in seminars on various issues of the day involving the United States and its international business environment.

From 2001 to 2009, Neil was active as President and CEO of a major German-owned sales and manufacturing subsidiary located in the Midwestern United States. His geographical area of responsibility included both North and South America. While he is now retired, he remains active in the business world, consulting to several CEOs of companies located in the United States.

A first-generation American, born of a Sicilian father and Scottish mother, he earned a BA degree with honors in International Relations from Stanford University. After a period of active duty in the U.S. Army Reserve, he earned an MBA from the Harvard Business School.